WALKING WISELY

WALKING WISELY

REAL GUIDANCE FOR LIFE'S JOURNEY

CHARLES STANLEY

NELSON IMPACT
A Division of Thomas Nelson Publishers
Since 1798

www.thomasnelson.com

Published by Nelson Impact, a Division of Thomas Nelson, Inc., P.O. Box 141000, Nashville, Tennessee, 37214.

ISBN: 1-4185-0587-0

Printed in the United States of America
05 06 07 – 9 8 7 6 5 4 3 2 1

CONTENTS

INTRODUCTION

If walking wisely were easy, more of us would do it.

This might seem like a harsh judgment, but it certainly seems to be true. Education—and the wisdom that supposedly comes with it—have long been prized above all else. For many years, here in America, we have had the finest educational system in the world. Other countries have now caught up and even surpassed us, at least in certain areas, but that simply makes the following statement more poignant.

> If the search for knowledge were sufficient unto itself, surely we would have solved all of the problems of mankind by now.

Unfortunately, most of the world looks inward, to itself, rather than outward to God, the only true source of all wisdom and understanding. Proverbs 4:5, 6 tells us:

Get wisdom! Get understanding!
>   Do not forget, nor turn away from the words of my mouth.
>   Do not forsake her, and she will preserve you;
>   Love her, and she will keep you (NKJV).

But what is this "wisdom" that will preserve and keep us? I believe that wisdom is the capacity to see things from God's perspective and to respond to them according to scriptural principles. In other words, wisdom is seeking heavenly opinions on earthly circumstances.

I would add only one condition to that statement—that "seeking" by itself is not enough. Application *must* follow acquisition. Wisdom involves seeking God's opinion, but it also involves doing what He suggests.

In this workbook, our goal is both to *seek* and to *apply* the divine wisdom of God, as revealed in His Word, His leadings, and His examples.

CHAPTER ONE

❖

THE CHALLENGE OF GOD'S WORD: WALK IN WISDOM

Who was the greatest artist in the Bible?

In my view, one of the most fascinating characters of all—and perhaps the most talented artist as well—is a little-known fellow who was commissioned by the Lord to *create*, out of the rawest of materials, the beautiful objects that God commanded the children of Israel to use when they worshiped Him in the tabernacle in the wilderness. These artifacts included the ark of the covenant, the bronze altar, and the seven-branch, six-foot-tall lampstand that stood in the inner court and provided the only light for that portion of the tabernacle.

The man's name was Bezalel, mentioned six times in the Book of Exodus, always with reference to the work God gave him to accomplish. Note this detailed description of just one of those items (Ex. 37:17–24):

> He [i.e., Bezalel] also made the lampstand of pure gold; of hammered
> work he made the lampstand. Its shaft, its branches, its bowls, its

1

ornamental knobs, and its flowers were of the *same piece*. And six branches came out of its sides: three branches of the lampstand out of one side, and three branches of the lampstand out of the other side. There were three bowls made like almond blossoms on one branch, with an ornamental knob and a flower, and three bowls made like almond blossoms on the other branch, with an ornamental knob and a flower—and so for the six branches coming out of the lampstand. And on the lampstand itself were four bowls made like almond blossoms, each with its ornamental knob and flower. There was a knob under the first two branches of the same, a knob under the second two branches of the same, and a knob under the third two branches of the same, according to the six branches extending from it. Their knobs and their branches were of one piece; *all of it was one hammered piece of pure gold.* And he made its seven lamps, its wicktrimmers, and its trays of pure gold. *Of a talent of pure gold* he made it, with all its utensils (NKJV).

Modern estimates of the weight of this masterpiece mention up to 150 pounds of pure gold. Even if we calculate the current market price of that much gold, the monetary value is not the emphasis for this point.

🔆 (BREAKOUT) STRAIGHT FROM THE BOOK . . .

God desires for our lives to bring glory to Him. God wants us to live in a way that causes others to want Christ Jesus in their lives. The foolish life does not bring glory to God; the wise life does.

Exodus 36:2 says that ". . . Moses called Bezalel and Aholiab, and every gifted artisan in whose heart the LORD had put *wisdom*, everyone whose heart was stirred, to come and do the work (NKJV, italics added).

From this verse two things can be deduced.

FIRST, wisdom comes from God and resides in the heart every bit as much as it resides in the mind.

SECOND, wisdom is not just mental and passive. It produces a physical counterpart that we might call *action*. Bezalel "came to do the work."

In other words, what's the point of having wisdom if we never use it, or as this study guide's title suggests, if we never *walk* in it?

We can identify five positive reasons God desires for us to walk in wisdom:

(1) God desires for us to become all that He created us to be.

(2) God desires for us to accomplish all of the work that He sets before us to do.

(3) God desires for us to receive, to experience, and to enjoy all the blessings He desires to pour into our lives.

(4) God desires for our lives to bring glory to Him.

(5) God desires that we avoid all the pitfalls associated with foolish living.

Let's work with the following table to see how various characters in the Bible either *did* or *did not* exemplify one or more of the reasons from the previous list. Several names and events are listed, but you could add many more. Don't be limited to a single event in any person's life. Consider, for example, any of several additional events in the lives of David, Samson, Moses, or any lesser-known characters as well. A good concordance (or Bible software) will take you immediately to any passages you might want to look up about any specific person or event, to jog your memory.

If you are part of a group, discuss with each other your reasons for assigning a plus (+) or a minus (–) to different events in the five categories of the chart

Two choices are filled out to show you how to work through the chart. Be aware that you don't need to assign a negative or positive value in every category for every person and event. Sometimes they simply do not apply.

Character	Event or Occurrence	Illustrates Reason #, + or —				
		1	2	3	4	5
David	The interlude with Bathsheba	—	—	—	—	—
Moses	Leading the Israelites out of Egypt	+	+	—	+	+
Paul	The shipwreck					
Stephen	His martyrdom					
Samson	Dalliance w/Delilah, to his death					
Daniel	In the lion's den					
Jephthah	Saving Israel; dealing w/daughter					
King Saul	Dealing with David					
Solomon	Dealing with 2 women/1 child					
Gideon	Conquering the Midianites					

❖ (Breakout) Straight from the Book . . .

Nothing man may acquire, earn, or achieve in the natural realm is as valuable as wisdom. One of the reasons God places such a high value on wisdom is no doubt because the stakes related to living wisely are so high.

LEARNING FROM OTHERS' MISTAKES

There's another list that's more or less the opposite of the first one—the list of reasons why people make *unwise* choices in life and thereby do not receive the blessings that God prefers to pour out upon them. This list includes the following:

(1) First, some foolish choices are made in ignorance.

(2) Second, some foolish choices are rooted in self-gratification.

(3) Third, some foolish choices are made in response to peer or societal pressure.

(4) Fourth, some foolish choices are made by those who believe that "I can live my life my way and win."

Let's illustrate each of these reasons for unwise choices:

Ignorance. Turn to Genesis 31:33, 34. These two verses tell what happened just as Leah and Rachel, the two daughters of Laban, were about to leave their father and go with Jacob, their husband, back to Jacob's homeland. Fill in the blank and answer the questions below.

> And Laban went into Jacob's tent, into Leah's tent, and into the two maids' tents, but he did not find them [i.e., his household idols]. Then he went out of Leah's tent and entered Rachel's tent. Now Rachel had taken the household idols, put them in the camel's saddle, and sat on them. And Laban _____ all about the tent but did not find them (NKJV).

1. I have heard it suggested that Rachel took her father's household Gods to spite her father for requiring Jacob to work seven extra years to win her hand. For this exercise let's reject that explanation. What, instead, could be a more likely reason

for what Rachel did? Put another way, why would Rachel feel that her father's household idols would have any value to her in her new home?

_____

_____

_____

2. How does God feel about the worship of idols?

_____

_____

_____

3. Is it possible that Rachel did not know enough about the true God to realize how serious a sin idol worship would be?

_____

_____

_____

4. What was the price of Rachel's lack of wisdom?

_____

_____

_____

5. What might have been the price if she had not been clever enough to fool her father? (Note: "Cleverness" and "wisdom" are not equal.)

_____

_____

_____

SELF-GRATIFICATION. Now, turn to Judges 16:17–19. These verses tell what happened to Samson after he had indulged himself with Delilah. Fill in the blanks and answer the questions below.

> [finally, Samson] . . . told her all his heart, and said to her, "No razor has ever come upon my head, for I have been a Nazirite to God from my mother's womb. If I am _____, then my strength will leave me, and I shall become weak, and be like any other man."
>
> . . . Delilah . . . sent and called for the lords of the Philistines, saying, "Come up once more, for he has told me all his heart." So the lords of the Philistines came up to her and brought the money in their hand. Then she _____ him to sleep on her knees, and called for a man and had him shave off the seven locks of his head. Then she began to _____ him, and his strength left him (NKJV).

1. Was it wise of Samson to tell Delilah the source of his strength?

_____

_____

_____

2. Why do you think he did it?

_____

_____

_____

3. What would have been the wiser course for him to follow, not just with Delilah but with other women whom the Bible tells us he "went in unto" as well?

_____

_____

_____

❊ (Breakout) How Can We Be Wiser than Our Major Weaknesses?

Several episodes from the life of Samson illustrate his major weakness, a strong drive for self-gratification, which Delilah (and others) was only too happy to satisfy. History teaches us, however, that Samson was not unique in that sense, for thousands of other men and women have come to grief through *unwise attempts* to satisfy their desires for physical gratification of all kinds.

Putting aside other powerful desires, such as the lust for power and riches, how can Christians fight against the obsession with sexual gratification that sometimes seems to dominate popular culture, both in America and throughout much of the world? This question is obviously not an easy one; millions of others have wrestled with it, too, and millions more wrestle with it at this very moment.

Think carefully about what you know the Bible says about misuse of sexuality. With that as background, identity some *wise, practical steps* Christians can take to protect themselves and their families. What wise course would you recommend for those who, like Samson, seem to have trouble resisting the world's major temptations? If you are in a group study, suggest that the group put together an "action list" that might be helpful on a daily basis.

_____

_____

_____

_____

_____

_____

_____

❈ (Breakout) Straight from the Book . . .

Any time a person limits the role of God in his life, or compromises God's commandments, that person is rejecting Him.

Peer or Societal Pressure. This next illustration can seem both amusing and horrifying at the same time. It can be amusing because these young people seem more typical of modern youth, having what they might have considered "innocent" fun, but it can also be horrifying because of the price they paid. However, we must remember that ridiculing or insulting a true Man of God, in ancient times, was a serious offense to God as well. God had just transferred the mantle of Elijah to Elisha, who was leaving Jericho after performing his first miracles.

Turn to 2 Kings 2:23, 24, fill in the blanks, and answer the question.

Then he [Elisha] went up from there to Bethel; and as he was going up the road, some youths came from the city and _____ him, and said to him, "Go up, you baldhead! Go up, you baldhead!"

So he turned around and looked at them, and pronounced a curse on them in the name of the LORD. And two female bears came out of the woods and _____ forty-two of the youths (2 Kin. 2:23, 24 NKJV).

1. What do you think the expression "Go up" means in this context?

_____

_____

2. If 42 youths were mauled, the group of mockers obviously included quite a number of people. Is it possible that Elisha's life might have been in danger?

_____

_____

3. If not, what else might justify the end result?

_____

_____

❖ (BREAKOUT) WHAT IS A NAZIRITE?

When Samson tells Delilah that he is a Nazirite (not to be confused with "Nazarene"), what does he mean? Numbers 6:1–21 explains in greater detail what the Nazirite vow entailed. It was a vow of dedication to God; the Nazirite set himself apart in service to the Lord.

Samson's Nazirite vow was permanent, required of him from birth. Many Bible scholars believe this was true of Samuel and John the Baptist as well, for like Samson, both were dedicated to the Lord "from the womb." A Nazirite from birth was forbidden to cut his hair for his entire life. Others, who usually would have taken the vow for a specified period of years, were required to shave their heads at the beginning, then to leave their hair uncut for the duration. They were also required to forsake all products of the grapevine—wine, raisins, and anything else made from the same plant, including grape leaves.

Some scholars believe that Paul took the same vow (Acts 21:24–26 and Acts 18). Read these passages and determine what you think.

Rebelliousness. Turn to Luke 15:13–16.

And not many days after, the younger son gathered all together, journeyed to a far country, and there _____ his possessions with prodigal living. But when he had spent all, there arose a severe famine in that land, and he began to be in want. Then he went and joined himself to a citizen of that country, and he sent him into his fields to feed _____. And he would gladly have filled his stomach with the pods that the swine ate, and no one gave him anything (NKJV).

1. This familiar story is often used to illustrate the love of God, always willing to forgive our prodigal ways and to welcome us into His arms. (Note: Continue reading to get to that part.) What does the passage say about our frequent inclination to rebel and about the assumption that we know better?

_____

_____

_____

2. What single word identifies what this young man lacked?

_____

_____

❖ (BREAKOUT) FOOLISH CHOICES OF OUR OWN

All of us have made foolish choices at one time or another. Dating the wrong person, going to the wrong party, taking the wrong road—some choices introduce people and events with long-lasting, negative influence into our lives. Other choices have no lasting effects and can even be funny. No one seems to escape foolish choices.

Review again the list of four common reasons for which people tend to make foolish choices. Then, in the four numbered spaces below, list one or two choices you've made for the corresponding reason. Then, after each item, *from hindsight*, indicate whether God might have been trying to help you make a wiser choice by encouraging you to listen more carefully to Him.

1. _____

_____

_____

2. _____

_____

_____

3. _____

_____

_____

4. _____

_____

_____

GOD DESIRES A BETTER WAY FOR US

Who said the following words, taken from First Kings 3:9? _____

> Therefore give to Your servant an understanding heart to judge Your people, that I may discern between good and evil. For who is able to judge this great people of Yours?" (NKJV)

Most readers, even if they cannot quote his exact words, will recognize the speaker as David's son, King Solomon. For thousands of years, Solomon has been known as the richest man who ever lived. Given the incredible fortunes some men have amassed in recent days, it's impossible to know whether Solomon still deserves that title—but only if you measure riches in monetary terms. However, great riches were never all that made Solomon unique: no man has ever been richer in wisdom.

The Lord answered Solomon's request (I Kin. 3:4) to an extent that we simply cannot comprehend. The mind of God is so vast—so far beyond our understanding—that even though He probably poured out upon Solomon only a *tiny portion* of His own wisdom, that small portion elevated Solomon well above all men.

Solomon *asked God* for wisdom. It took some amount of initiative to make that request in the first place, but can we not do the same for ourselves? Does God not promise, over and over, to give us wisdom if we ask?

Indeed . . .

> We must choose to pursue wisdom.
> We must seek God's plan.
> We must take responsibility for applying wisdom to our lives.

WORDS TO REMEMBER . . .

If any of you lacks wisdom, let him ask of God, who gives to all liberally and without reproach, and it will be given to him (James 1:5 NKJV).

CLOSING PRAYER . . .

Our Father, we pray that You would pour out Your wisdom upon us,
for we recognize that we cannot be wise in our own strength. Help us not
to listen to our own impulses and our own appetites, but to the voice of
Your Holy Spirit, guiding and directing every aspect of our lives.
In Jesus' name, Amen.

❈ (BREAKOUT) STRAIGHT FROM THE BOOK . . .

No area of life is beyond the need for wisdom, off-limits to God's wisdom, or ignored by God's Word. God's wisdom can be readily applied to every decision or choice we make, every relationship we have, every emotion we feel, every action we take, every opinion we hold, and every idea or challenge we pursue.

CHAPTER TWO

EARTHLY WISDOM VERSUS GODLY WISDOM

One of the more popular entertainments here in America is a good, old-fashioned disaster movie. You could even look at our passion for hurricanes, earthquakes, tornadoes, fires, and slime-pit creatures that destroy whole cities and conclude that Americans are obsessed with calamities.

Perhaps one of the most fascinating movies that has never been made would tell the story of a gigantic biblical disaster that literally changed the world.

(BREAKOUT) STRAIGHT FROM THE BOOK . . .

Discernment is especially important in crisis times. Even ungodly people will admit that in times of crisis or natural catastrophe, people don't think clearly. Our perception becomes clouded when we are under intense emotional pressure or time constraints. It is in times of crisis that we especially need the discerning power of the Holy Spirit at work in our lives.

Let's look at what happened, and then let's look at another project of the same general type and identify some differences. Read Genesis 11:1–9, fill in the blanks below, and then answer the questions that follow.

> Now the whole earth had one language and one speech. And it came to pass, as they _____ from the east, that they found a plain in the land of Shinar, and they dwelt there. Then they said to one another, "Come, let us make bricks and bake them thoroughly." They had brick for stone, and they had asphalt for mortar. And they said, "Come, let us build ourselves a city, and a tower whose top is in the heavens; let us make a name for ourselves, lest we be _____ abroad over the face of the whole earth."
>
> But the LORD came down to see the city and the tower which the sons of men had built. And the LORD said, "Indeed the people are one and they all have one language, and this is what they begin to do; now nothing that they propose to do will be withheld from them. Come, let Us go down and there _____ their language, that they may not understand one another's speech." So the LORD scattered them abroad from there over the face of all the earth, and they ceased building the city. Therefore its name is called Babel, because there the LORD confused the language of all the earth; and from there the LORD scattered them abroad over the face of all the earth (NKJV).

1. Why did God become so angry with the people who were building the tower?[1]

   _____

   _____

   _____

2. What prior command, issued by God in Genesis 1:28, were these people directly disobeying?

_____

_____

_____

3. What kind of wisdom were they basing their activities on? (Refer to the list of 4 non-wise motivators in chapter 1.)

_____

_____

_____

Read 1 Kings 6:11–14, a contrast to all these passages:

> Then the word of the LORD came to Solomon, saying: "Concerning this temple which you are building, if you walk in My statutes, execute My judgments, keep all My commandments, and walk in them, then I will perform My word with you, which I spoke to your father David. And I will dwell among the children of Israel, and will not forsake My people Israel."
> So Solomon built the temple and finished it (NKJV).

To get the whole story of Solomon's temple, read the complete chapter, plus chapters before and after. Even though verses 11–14 tell only a tiny portion of the story, they give us very important information.

1. Why was God so pleased with Solomon, and what were His conditions for _remaining_ pleased?

_____

_____

_____

2. What promise did God make to David that this temple fulfilled? (Refer to 2 Samuel 7:8–16.)

_____

_____

_____

_____

3. What kind of wisdom was Solomon basing his activity on?

_____

_____

_____

_____

(BREAKOUT) REFLECTION AND RESPONSE

If you take two magnets and put the opposite poles (i.e., the "positive" and the "negative" ends) close together, they will repel each other. The expression, "polar opposites," comes from this phenomenon. Sometimes it seems that many people who choose earthly wisdom over godly wisdom are turning *away* from God and getting as far from Him as they can.

It often seems that if God and His wisdom were at the North Pole, many people would automatically head for the South Pole. Again—the polar opposite.

Keeping that concept in mind, reflect on your own experience. Then, in the first column below, list three or four of the main reasons you believe many people choose to turn away from God and toward human understanding. In the second column, list the polar (i.e., Godly) opposite of each of those reasons. Which do you choose?

We choose earthly wisdom out of	Polar Opposite
_____	_____
_____	_____
_____	_____
_____	_____
_____	_____

THE GODLY WISDOM EQUATION

Obviously, two different kinds of wisdom were at play in the tower and the temple examples above. The first is *earthly* wisdom, and the second is *godly* wisdom. However, as the history of the world makes clear over and over again, apart from God a human being simply cannot function in true wisdom. So what is this "godly" wisdom?

Fill in the blanks for Proverbs 9:10: "_____ _____ _____ _____ _____ _____ _____ _____ _____ _____."

Fear, in this verse refers to *reverence*. Those who fear God stand in awe of Him. Now, look at the second half of the same verse, seldom quoted in its entirety, which says: "And the knowledge of the Holy One is understanding." In other words:

1. "Fear of the LORD" in the first half of the verse means *honor* and *respect* for Him.

2. *Honor and respect* can only be based on *knowledge* of Him.

3. *Knowledge* leads to *understanding*.

4. *Understanding* leads to *wisdom*!

The whole formula might be expressed as:

FEARING AND KNOWING = UNDERSTANDING AND WISDOM

Perhaps this simplified formula could be called the "Godly Wisdom Equation."

(BREAKOUT) THINK IT THROUGH AGAIN!

Do you believe that many people choose earthly wisdom over godly wisdom as a conscious decision? For some, it seems to be more of a *default* decision, brought about by a simple failure to search out and actively seek the wisdom of God. In turn, this lack of strategy often seems to be based on the failure to realize that our God is a *personal* God who wants to guide and sustain us in every aspect of our lives.

In that context, "The fear of the LORD is the beginning of wisdom," from the first half of Proverbs 9:10 gives us two concepts to deal with: "fear of the Lord" and "wisdom." We already know that the word *beginning*, in this case, means *precondition* or *prerequisite*—you have to have *one* before you can have *the other*!

Why? Why can't you have wisdom without restrictions? In what ways can the "fear of the Lord" concept often be misunderstood? Should we be truly afraid of God?

Beyond that, how does "fear of the LORD" relate to our understanding of our loving God as both *personal* and *intimate* if we also say that He *demands respect*? Is it possible that some people, in their worldly wisdom, have confused the terms and turned *respect for God* into a negative concept?

_____

_____

_____

_____

_____

_____

_____

The following scriptural passages are just three among many that illustrate both sides of the Godly Wisdom Equation we previously formulated. Look up the verses, fill in the blanks, and answer the questions below.

> So Moses said to him [i.e., Pharaoh], "As soon as I have gone out of the city, I will _____ out my hands to the LORD; the thunder will _____, and there will be no more hail, that you may know that the earth is the LORD's. But as for you and your servants, I know that you will not yet fear the LORD God" (Ex. 9:29, 30 NKJV).

> Then those who _____ the LORD spoke to one another, And the LORD listened and heard them; So a book of remembrance was _____ before Him For those who fear the LORD And who meditate on His name (Mal. 3:16 NKJV).

> Then the churches throughout all Judea, Galilee, and Samaria had peace and were edified. And _____ in the fear of the Lord and in the _____ of the Holy Spirit, they were multiplied (Acts 9:31 NKJV).

1. What *concept* do all three of these verses illustrate—that we should *do what* with respect to the Lord?

   _____

   _____

   _____

   _____

2. In which of the three examples did someone *wisely fear* the Lord?

   _____

   _____

   _____

   _____

3. In which did someone NOT *wisely fear* the Lord?

   _____

   _____

   _____

   _____

4. Knowing what you know of biblical history (for the complete stories are not told in these brief verses), what can you deduce from the first example about someone's failure to fear the Lord?

   _____

   _____

   _____

   _____

(Breakout) The Godly Wisdom Equation

General Response

What do you consider the most difficult part of the Godly Wisdom Equation for most people: the "godly fear" or the "wisdom and knowledge" aspect?

Personal Response

What has been the most difficult part for you? Why?

(Breakout) Straight from the Book . . .

The Bible declares, Get wisdom! Get understanding! (Prov. 4:5). The two are not the same.

The Four Main Errors of Earthly Wisdom

Proverbs 28:26 says, "He who trusts in his own heart is a fool, But whoever walks wisely will be delivered" (NKJV). Isaiah 55:8, 9 also says: "My thoughts are not your thoughts, nor are your ways My ways . . . For as the heavens are higher than the earth, so are My ways higher than your ways" (NKJV).

Trusting in our own hearts is another way of saying that we put our faith in our own abilities rather than relying on the infinite resources of God—*all of which are higher than ours.* We do this in four main ways, believing that

1. wisdom is limited to the mind of man;

2. wisdom is based on what can be perceived by the five human senses;

3. wisdom is doing what man collectively defines as rational or provable;

4. wisdom is doing "whatever works."

Several Scriptures are listed in the table below. The Scriptures summarize the story of a biblical character who made one or more of the four mistakes listed above, regarding personal earthly wisdom. Read the selections, identify the main character(s), and indicate which mistake(s) each one made. Add as many examples as you like and then answer the questions that follow.

Scripture	Main Characters and Story	Mistake(s)
(1) Numbers 22:22–32	Balaam beats his donkey	1, 2, 3, 4
(2) Matthew 26:14–16	Judas and his betrayal	4 (and others?)
(3) Luke 1:5–20	Zacharias and his doubts	1, 2, 3, 4
(4) Judges 4:18–21	Jael killed by Sisera	2, 4
(5) Matthew 7:26, 27	Man who built his house upon sand	4

It's much easier to analyze the past than to predict the future. It is also much easier to be wise in hindsight than "in the moment."

Think carefully about the five examples in the preceding table. Then try to identify, in each case, what would have changed both the responses of the people involved and the outcomes of their stories, *if they'd had God's infinite knowledge and wisdom.*

1. _____
   _____
   _____
   _____
   _____

2. _____
   _____
   _____
   _____
   _____

3. _____
   _____
   _____
   _____
   _____

4. _____
   _____
   _____
   _____
   _____

5. _____

   _____

   _____

   _____

   _____

❖ (BREAKOUT) STRAIGHT FROM THE BOOK . . .

The world says that wisdom is based upon what a person can perceive with his natural senses. God's wisdom calls for a person to walk in the discerning power of the Holy Spirit, who is not at all limited by human senses.

WE MUST CHOOSE GOD'S WISDOM

God's wisdom involves discernment far beyond our five senses. As with salvation itself, God's wisdom is never forced upon us. We must purposely choose salvation, and we must purposely choose His wisdom. We must invite God to lead us to His way and to His plan. As we do so we must ask ourselves continually

> am I wisely using my talents, time, and resources?
> am I wisely taking this action in this relationship?
> am I wisely living out the purpose God has for my life?

As you ask these questions in your own life, look and listen for God's response. Ask for God's wisdom even as you pray, "Lord, please give me Your answer."

In the words of Christ Himself, "Ask, and you will receive, that your joy may be full" (John 16:24 NKJV).

Wisdom would do no less.

WORDS TO REMEMBER . . .

Who is wise and understanding among you? Let him show by good conduct that his works are done in the meekness of wisdom. But if you have bitter envy and self-seeking in your hearts, do not boast and lie against the truth. This wisdom does not descend from above, but is earthly, sensual, demonic. For where envy and self-seeking exist, confusion and every evil thing are there. But the wisdom that is from above is first pure, then peaceable, gentle, willing to yield, full of mercy and good fruits, without partiality and without hypocrisy (James 3:13–17 NKJV).

CLOSING PRAYER . . .

Our Father, we pray that You might help us learn to rely on Your wisdom rather than our own. We acknowledge the weaknesses of our hearts and minds, and praise You for the infinite wisdom, grace, and mercy that all proceed from Your heavenly throne. Protect us not only through Your might but through Your limitless knowledge and understanding of all things.

In Jesus' name, Amen.

(BREAKOUT) STRAIGHT FROM THE BOOK . . .

The world and God's Word present two very different views of wisdom. From God's perspective, earthly wisdom—human or natural wisdom—is grounded in man's fallen nature. Godly wisdom—divine or spiritual wisdom—is based upon man's "new nature" given at the time of a person's spiritual rebirth (2 Cor. 5:17 NKJV).

✳ (Breakout) Is Common Wisdom Ever Uncommon?

We have identified four main errors of earthly wisdom:

1. making foolish choices in ignorance;

2. making foolish choices for self-gratification;

3. making foolish choices in response to peer or societal pressure;

4. making foolish choices in the belief that we can live our lives "our" way and win.

Now, think back to all the "great quotations" you've heard down through the years that support these four main errors. For example, one of the most famous, "I think, therefore I am" by Rene Descartes, actually supports all four. This quotation was verified in great detail by the longer Descartes commentary from which it came.

However, it isn't necessary to concentrate only on famous quotations. What common expressions that you hear often support one or more of these four errors? Relate these expressions to the four main errors and list them below:

1. _____

_____

_____

2. _____

_____

_____

3. _____

_____

_____

4. _____

_____

_____

Can you think of any non-biblical great quotations or common expressions of wisdom that avoid all four of the main errors of earthly wisdom?

1. _____

_____

_____

2. _____

_____

_____

3. _____

_____

_____

EIGHT AMAZINGLY WONDERFUL BENEFITS OF WISDOM

I once knew a young man named Kenny, who was obsessed with auto racing. His parents desperately tried to keep him in the classroom. However, the minute he turned sixteen he was ready to quit so he could hang out at the local track eighteen hours a day. His parents barely managed to get him through high school.

Meanwhile, Kenny's love for racing evolved into a passion for engine and chassis design. By the time he reached eighteen he knew that he wanted to be an automotive engineer. However, by then his grades were so bad he had little hope of getting into college; he took a low-level job at the track just to stay close to what he called "the game."

In time, largely because of his hustle and his mechanical skills, he landed a beginner's spot on one of the NASCAR teams. Soon he captured the attention of one of the sport's moneyed backstage people who saw potential in Kenny beyond what anyone else had spotted. The man pulled strings and offered financial aid, and eventually Kenny went off to college to study engineering.

Amazingly, Kenny did far better than anyone thought he could and even graduated with honors. In fact, his undergrad work got him a lot of attention, and suddenly he found himself the darling of a half-dozen automotive companies and racing teams. What to do?

For a while, Kenny agonized back and forth between the two best offers. One came from a racing team whose main owner was a Christian businessman (not the one who sent him to college), who saw Kenny almost as a son. Kenny would have started at the bottom, at a smaller salary, but the way eventually would lead to a top position in the field he loved. He often would work "in the pits" with some of the best in the business.

The other team was owned by a huge conglomerate. To everyone's surprise, Kenny accepted this offer even though it pulled him away from the track and put him at corporate headquarters. Why? Perhaps it was because he'd come so close to missing out altogether. Kenny was married by that time and had convinced himself that he needed to concentrate on his future security. The bigger company offered a better package of medical and investment benefits than the first team, and it promised him that eventually he could get back to the hands-on action at the track.

Kenny became a corporate designer and then a department manager. Though he visits the racetrack often, many years later he has still never spent a working day "in the pits" to see firsthand how his designs work in real life. Rumor has it that he drinks quite a bit and sometimes seems very bitter.

WHAT ARE EARTHLY BENEFITS WORTH?

Kenny's story would not ordinarily be called an American tragedy. On the contrary, he was considered a huge success by those who knew his work—but not by his heart.

It may well be that the one thing we miss the most when we trade earthly wisdom for godly wisdom and heavenly benefits for earthly benefits is the Lord's infinite ability to know our hearts at the most intimate level. Only God, in His infinite love, can orchestrate the whole universe and bring into our lives the things most likely to satisfy us at the deepest levels of our being. Everything else is second best.

When we turn our lives over to God and trust exclusively in His wisdom, at least eight major heavenly benefits result from an intimate relationship with Him:

BENEFIT #1: a gain in our knowledge of God,

BENEFIT #2: clear guidance from God,

BENEFIT #3: God's divine protection,

BENEFIT #4: God's power and strength,

BENEFIT #5: genuine joy and contentment,

BENEFIT #6: a good self-image,

BENEFIT #7: whole-person prosperity,

BENEFIT #8: good health and a long life.

Let's examine these benefits one-by-one and see how they are manifested in the lives of real people.

BENEFIT 1: A GAIN IN OUR KNOWLEDGE OF GOD

The Scripture references in the following table give evidence of fifteen attributes of God. *Knowing about* God is not the same as *knowing God from personal experience,* and recognizing even a few of His attributes can give you a good start toward experiencing Him. **Select two or more Scriptures** from each entry in the reference table below, and then write the attribute of God that you discover.

SCRIPTURES	ATTRIBUTE OF GOD
Gen. 1:1; Ps. 8; Acts 17:24–27; Col. 1:15–17; Heb. 1:1–3	
Gen. 17:1; Ex. 6:3; Num. 24:4; Ps. 91:1; Is. 13:6; Rev. 1:8; 4:8; 11:17	
Is. 6:3; Lev. 11:44; Josh. 24:19; 1 Pet. 1:15, 16; Rev. 15:4; 4:8	
1 Sam. 16:7; Ps. 139:1–4, 23, 24; Jer. 17:10; Matt. 6:8, 18, 32; 10:30; John 1:48, 49; 2:25; 6:64	
Ps. 139:5–12; Matt. 18:20; 28:20	
Gen. 6:5–7; Ex. 34:7; Deut. 10:17, 18; 32:4; Ps. 11:7; Rom. 2:4–11; Heb. 10:30; 1 Pet. 1:17	
Gen. 21:33; Ps. 90:1–2; 102:27, 28; Is. 40:28	
Num. 14:21; Deut. 10:17; Ps. 8:1; 104:1; Is. 6:1–3; 57:15; Matt. 16:27; John 1:14; 17:5; 1 Tim. 6:14–16; Rev. 4:11	
Ex. 34:6; Ps. 103:8–13; Mic. 7:18; John 3:16–18; Titus 1:2	
Rom. 11:33, 34; 1 Cor. 2:6, 7; 1 Tim. 6:16 Rom. 1:19, 20; 2:14, 15; Acts 14:17; 17:26, 27	
Ex. 33:20–23; John 1:18; Col. 1:15; 1 Tim. 1:17; 6:16; 1 John 4:12, 20	
Ps. 118:1; 136; 36:7, 9; 63:3, 4; 34:8; 31:19	
Deut. 7:9; 32:4; Josh. 23:14–16; Titus 1:2; Ps. 117; 118:1–4; Ex. 34:6; 2 Tim. 2:13; 1 John 1:9	
Num. 14:18; Neh. 9:16–21; Ps. 103:8; Rom. 9:22, 23; 2 Pet. 3:9	

As you walk in the wisdom of the Lord, you'll know more about what to expect because all the attributes that were part of God eons ago, are part of Him today, and will be part of Him throughout eternity.

✣ (Breakout) Straight from the Book . . .

The more we come to know God, the more we are going to learn the way God works, the things God desires to do in our lives and in the lives of others, and the plans God has made for mankind's eternal good. We are going to feel God's heartbeat.

✣ (Breakout) Moses and His Encounters with God

Of all the characters in the Bible, the only one who had a well-documented, ongoing, personal, face-to-face relationship with God was Moses. Abraham was called a "friend of God," but we have little record of conversations between them. In later years, David also heard from God fairly often, but by then God had begun to speak primarily through His appointed prophets. Moses was unique, and his personal knowledge of God was unique as well.

On one occasion, Moses even gathered his courage and asked to *see* God, who until that point had remained invisible. God could not allow that to happen, of course—His glory is literally too magnificent for us humans to behold with our physical eyes in our sinful states. However, because Moses trusted God and had walked with Him so closely, God protected Moses by putting him in a cleft of the rock on Mount Sinai, covering his eyes while He passed by, then allowing Moses a quick glimpse of Himself from behind.

Before God did these things, He spoke to Moses and gave him what are often called the Thirteen Attributes of God. After reading the text, identify and list from this passage the attributes that are often assigned to God.

And the LORD passed before him and proclaimed, "The LORD, the LORD God, merciful and gracious, longsuffering, and abounding in goodness and truth, keeping mercy for thousands, forgiving iniquity and transgression and sin, by no means clearing the guilty, visiting the iniquity of the fathers upon the children and the children's children to the third and fourth generation" (Ex. 34:6, 7 NKJV).

_____ _____ _____

_____ _____ _____

_____ _____ _____

_____ _____ _____

_____ _____ _____

BENEFIT 2: CLEAR GUIDANCE FROM GOD

The following biblical extract gives us an example of what happens when God offers us His wisdom and we refuse to accept it or act on it. Many people know the story of Cain and Abel, but not everyone remembers the background before Cain killed his brother. Read Genesis 4:6–8, fill in the blanks below, and then answer the questions.

So the LORD said to Cain, "Why are you angry? And why has your countenance _____? If you do well, will you not be accepted? And if you do not do well, sin lies at the door. And its desire is for you, but you should _____ _____ it."

Now Cain talked with Abel his brother; and it came to pass, when they were in the field, that Cain rose up against Abel his brother and _____ him (NKJV).

1. Did God have clear knowledge of what was in Cain's heart?

   _____

   _____

   _____

2. Was His advice sound?

   _____

   _____

   _____

3. Did Cain accept or reject God's advice?

   _____

   _____

   _____

4. Read Genesis 4:1–5. Why was Cain so angry, and what do you believe he might have done differently to make positive changes in the situation?

   _____

   _____

   _____

❖ (BREAKOUT) HOW DOES GOD KNOW WHAT HE KNOWS?

This side of heaven we will never understand many things about God, given the limits of human knowledge and comprehension. However, one of God's remarkable abilities can be explained in general terms, even if we don't understand the how of it at all.

Many people seem to confuse *knowledge* with *cause* regarding God's understanding of the future. God's understanding of what will happen tomorrow doesn't mean that He therefore must have caused it. Instead, it is quite likely that God invented time for our convenience. God has no requirement for time whatsoever; He exists in eternity, outside of earthly time, and is therefore able to view the past, the present, and the future simultaneously, as one continuous scene.

Even though He can step in at any time He chooses, He can see what's coming tomorrow even as He can see what happened yesterday, without being the direct *cause*. On the other hand, for example, He always has the option of granting your prayer request for the means to pay your rent, made by you the night before it's due, by "reminding" a vendor who has owed you money to send you a check that will arrive tomorrow.

(BREAKOUT) HOW DID CAIN KILL HIS BROTHER?

Even though the biblical text contains no reference whatsoever to any specific instrument of death, many seem to believe that Cain picked up a rock and crashed it against Abel's skull. However, several elements within the text could suggest otherwise.

For example, when God said to Cain that "sin is crouching at your door," could He have been suggesting that Cain was thinking about something he shouldn't have been considering? If so, there might be an implication that the act of murder was not an act of sudden, unanticipated passion. Could He also have been implying that Cain might be thinking about a method and a weapon, in advance?

Some Hebrew language scholars believe that the wording of Genesis 4:8

in the original text suggests that Cain killed Abel in the same way that a ritual sacrifice would be conducted. A sacrifice of that kind, during biblical times, always required the spilling and complete draining of the blood—for the life of the animal was in the blood. Now note what God said to Cain in Genesis 4:10, 11.

> And He said, "What have you done? The voice of your brother's blood cries out to Me from the ground. So now you are cursed from the earth, which has opened its mouth to receive your brother's blood from your hand (NKJV).

A wound caused by a rock to the skull would not necessarily cause bleeding. Almost certainly it would not produce lots of bleeding, and it absolutely would not drain the body of all its blood. A quick, intentional cut across the throat, as with a sacrificial animal, would.

This subject is not particularly pleasant to think about, but perhaps looking at it this way can give us additional insight into what might have happened.

BENEFIT 3: GOD'S DIVINE PROTECTION

The Bible abounds with stories of God's divine protection over His people. Daniel in the lion's den is certainly one of the most familiar examples. The story of Paul and the poisonous viper is probably not as well-known, but both stories illustrate how God often pairs His protection of us with something else. Read Daniel 6:10; 16–20 and fill in the blanks.

> Now when Daniel knew that the writing [i.e., a new ordinance enacted by Daniel's enemies, commanding that all people pray only to the king] was _____ he went home. And in his upper room,

with his windows open toward Jerusalem, he knelt down on his knees three times that day, and prayed and gave thanks before his God, as was his custom since early days. . . .

So the king gave the command, and they brought Daniel and _____ him into the den of lions. But the king spoke, saying to Daniel, "Your God, whom you serve continually, He will _____ you." Then a stone was brought and laid on the mouth of the den, and the king sealed it with his own signet ring and with the signets of his lords, that the purpose concerning Daniel might not be changed.

Now the king went to his palace and spent the night fasting; and no musicians were brought before him. Also his sleep went from him. Then the king arose very early in the morning and went in haste to the den of lions. And when he came to the den, he cried out with a _____ voice to Daniel. The king spoke, saying to Daniel, "Daniel, servant of the living God, has your God, whom you serve _____, been able to deliver you from the lions?" (NKJV)

Now read Acts 28:3–6, fill in the blanks, and then answer the questions relating to *both* of these examples.

But when Paul had gathered a bundle of sticks and laid them on the fire, a viper came out because of the heat, and _____ on his hand. So when the natives saw the creature hanging from his hand, they said to one another, "No doubt this man is a murderer, whom, though he has escaped the sea, yet justice does not allow to live." But he _____ _____ the creature into the fire and suffered no harm. However, they were expecting that he would swell up or suddenly fall down dead. But after they had _____ for a long time and saw no harm come to him, they changed their minds and said that he was a god (NKJV).

1. Who protected Daniel and Paul from harm?

   _____

   _____

2. When the ordinance against praying to anyone but the king went out, what did Daniel do?

   _____

   _____

   _____

   _____

3. When Paul shook the snake off into the fire, who was watching?

   _____

   _____

4. What was the common reaction to what God did for His people in these two stories?

   _____

   _____

   _____

   _____

5. How is God's protection of us often used by Him for His divine purposes?

   _____

   _____

   _____

   _____

BENEFIT 4: GOD'S POWER AND STRENGTH

The Bible abounds with mighty demonstrations and unbreakable promises of God's power and strength. The demonstrations begin with creation itself and the promises extend all the way through the final events of Revelation. Let's look at just two lesser known, but utterly spectacular, examples from the Book of Joshua.

Read Joshua 3:14–17 and fill in the blanks:

> So it was, when the people set out from their camp to _____ over the Jordan, with the priests bearing the ark of the covenant before the people, and as those who bore the ark came to the Jordan, and the feet of the priests who bore the ark _____ in the edge of the water (for the Jordan overflows all its banks during the whole time of harvest), that the waters which came down from upstream stood still, and rose in a heap very far away at Adam, the city that is beside Zaretan. So the waters that went down into the Sea of the Arabah, the Salt Sea, failed, and were cut off; and the people crossed over opposite Jericho. Then the priests who bore the ark of the covenant of the LORD stood firm on dry ground in the midst of the Jordan; and all Israel _____ _____ on dry ground, until all the people had crossed completely over the Jordan (NKJV).

❈ (BREAKOUT) STRAIGHT FROM THE BOOK . . .

Never lose sight of the fact that God sees the totality of your life. He knows you inside and out. He knows your thoughts, your feelings, your physical makeup. He knows your past, your present, and your future. He knows your natural talents, your experiences, your spiritual gifts. God sees the whole of who you are, what you are called to do, and what you are facing right now.

Read Joshua 10:12–14, fill in the blanks, and then answer the questions.

> Then Joshua spoke to the LORD in the day when the LORD delivered up the Amorites before the children of Israel, and he said in the sight of Israel:
>
> "Sun, stand still over Gibeon; And Moon, in the Valley of Aijalon." So the sun _____ _____, And the moon _____, Till the people had revenge Upon their enemies.
>
> Is this not written in the Book of Jasher? So the sun stood still in the midst of heaven, and did not hasten to go down for about a whole day. And there has been no day like that, before it or after it, that the LORD _____ the voice of a man; for the LORD fought for Israel (NKJV).

1. Both of these examples show the awesome power of God over what?

   _____

   _____

   _____

2. In both cases, who benefited from what God did?

   _____

   _____

   _____

3. What kind of relationship did the person (or people) in both of these examples have with God?

   _____

   _____

   _____

4. Was it a new relationship, or had it been developed over the course of time?

_____

_____

_____

5. Did the person (or people) involved always honor their responsibilities to that relationship?

_____

_____

_____

6. Did God always honor His responsibilities?

_____

_____

_____

7. What do you conclude about how God uses His power and strength? For whose benefit? When and under what conditions?

_____

_____

_____

_____

_____

BENEFIT 5: GENUINE JOY AND CONTENTMENT

When I began to pull this section together I tried to think of all the biblical characters who attained joy and contentment within their personal lives, as a direct result of walking wisely with the Lord. Almost all of those biblical characters who had any relationship with God at all attained joy and contentment within their personal lives as a direct result of walking wisely with the Lord. Sometimes they caused themselves sorrow and loss as well.

(BREAKOUT) STRAIGHT FROM THE BOOK . . .

God desires to protect us from all things that are evil—from substances that do us harm, from situations that are dangerous, from environments that are deadly, from circumstances that can destroy us. God's wisdom leads us as far away from evil as possible.

David is the classic example. Certainly he brought grief, misery, and disappointment upon both himself and his people, but he also knew genuine joy and contentment after he turned to the Lord and walked in God's wisdom. Given all that, perhaps the blessings of *Benefit #5* might best be illustrated by a series of scripture quotations containing direct references to *joy and contentment*. Many of these would apply to every biblical character from Adam to Jude. Your challenge is to read through each one and indicate, in the column on the right, *which of the verses also apply to you*.

CHECK THE LAST COLUMN IF THESE SCRIPTURES APPLY TO YOU . . .	YES
Not that I speak in regard to need, for I have learned in whatever state I am, to be **content** (Phil. 4:11 NKJV).	
Not that we have dominion over your faith, but are fellow workers for your **joy**; for by faith you stand (2 Cor. 1:24 NKJV).	
Until now you have asked nothing in My name. Ask, and you will receive, that your **joy** may be full (John 16:24 NKJV).	
Now may the God of hope fill you with all **joy** and peace in believing, that you may abound in hope by the power of the Holy Spirit (Rom. 15:13 NKJV).	

Check the Last Column if These Scriptures Apply to You . . .	Yes
For what is our hope, or **joy**, or crown of rejoicing? Is it not even you in the presence of our Lord Jesus Christ at His coming? (1 Thess. 2:19 NKJV)	
And having food and clothing, with these we shall be **content** (1 Tim. 6:8 NKJV).	
But the fruit of the Spirit is love, **joy**, peace, longsuffering, kindness, goodness, faithfulness, gentleness, self-control. Against such there is no law. And those who are Christ's have crucified the flesh with its passions and desires. If we live in the Spirit, let us also walk in the Spirit (Gal. 5:22–25 NKJV).	
Rejoice in that day and leap for **joy**! For indeed your reward is great in heaven, For in like manner their fathers did to the prophets (Luke 6:23 NKJV).	
You have made known to me the ways of life; You will make me full of **joy** in Your presence (Acts 2:28 NKJV).	

Did you score 100% in the above exercise? If not, this might be an excellent time to speak to the Lord and make it clear that you desire to accept His sovereignty and walk in His wisdom from this moment forward.

BENEFIT 6: A GOOD SELF-IMAGE

One of my favorite biblical illustrations of a good self-image deals with the two prophets Elijah and Elisha, near the end of Elijah's life. God was about to take Elijah directly to heaven (he and Enoch were the only two men in the Bible who were given that honor), and He seemed to be determined that Elisha should "give Him space" in his last moments on planet Earth. The point is to show how relentless Elisha was in pursuing what he wanted, despite repeated attempts by others to discourage him. Persistence isn't always proof of a good self-image, but in this case (and also, given his instant willingness to follow Elijah in the beginning and to burn his equipment to boil his oxen so that he literally could not go back to the plow, 1 Kin. 19:19–21), it seems to earn a commendation. This selection is a bit longer than most, but it's a fast read. Read 2 Kings 2:1–14 and answer the questions that follow.

(Breakout) Straight from the Book . . .

When we seek divine wisdom, God imparts to us the ability to see a situation from His perspective, which is this: He has strength and ability to compensate for every area of weakness we have. He enables us to do what we cannot do in our own strength. The person who is walking wisely comes to the conclusion, "There's nothing too big . . . too difficult . . . too problematic for God to handle."

And it came to pass, when the LORD was about to take up Elijah into heaven by a whirlwind, that Elijah went with Elisha from Gilgal. Then Elijah said to Elisha, "Stay here, please, for the LORD has sent me on to Bethel."

But Elisha said, "As the LORD lives, and as your soul lives, I will not leave you!" So they went down to Bethel.

Now the sons of the prophets who were at Bethel came out to Elisha, and said to him, "Do you know that the LORD will take away your master from over you today?"

And he said, "Yes, I know; keep silent!"

Then Elijah said to him, "Elisha, stay here, please, for the LORD has sent me on to Jericho."

But he said, "As the LORD lives, and as your soul lives, I will not leave you!" So they came to Jericho.

Now the sons of the prophets who were at Jericho came to Elisha and said to him, "Do you know that the LORD will take away your master from over you today?"

So he answered, "Yes, I know; keep silent!"

Then Elijah said to him, "Stay here, please, for the LORD has sent me on to the Jordan."

But he said, "As the LORD lives, and as your soul lives, I will not leave you!" So the two of them went on. And fifty men of the sons of the prophets went and stood facing them at a distance, while the two of them stood by the Jordan. Now Elijah took his mantle, rolled it up, and struck the water; and it was divided this way and that, so that the two of them crossed over on dry ground.

And so it was, when they had crossed over, that Elijah said to Elisha, "Ask! What may I do for you, before I am taken away from you?"

Elisha said, "Please let a double portion of your spirit be upon me."

So he said, "You have asked a hard thing. Nevertheless, if you see me when I am taken from you, it shall be so for you; but if not, it shall not be so." Then it happened, as they continued on and talked, that suddenly a chariot of fire appeared with horses of fire, and separated the two of them; and Elijah went up by a whirlwind into heaven.

And Elisha saw it, and he cried out, "My father, my father, the chariot of Israel and its horsemen!" So he saw him no more. And he took hold of his own clothes and tore them into two pieces. He also took up the mantle of Elijah that had fallen from him, and went back and stood by the bank of the Jordan. Then he took the mantle of Elijah that had fallen from him, and struck the water, and said, "Where is the LORD God of Elijah?" And when he also had struck the water, it was divided this way and that; and Elisha crossed over (NKJV).

✂ (BREAKOUT) WHY THE "TEARING OF THE CLOTHES"?

The Bible records a number of cases in which someone "tore his clothes," "rent his garments," or otherwise performed various levels of mayhem on what he was wearing. In an age when you couldn't drive down to the local shopping mall and replace ruined clothes in a heartbeat, why would someone do such a thing?

The answer lies within an understanding of ancient customs. Understood by all, the tearing of the clothes was a graphic demonstration of grief or dismay. Thus, though it surely caused all kinds of replacement problems in comparison to what might happen today, in that era it was an honored (even "required") custom and not the least bit strange.

In effect, they were saying, "These are the clothes I was wearing when I heard the news, and I don't ever want to be caught wearing them again!"

1. What words did Elisha repeat each time Elijah tried to get him to stay where he was and let Elijah go on alone?

   _____

   _____

   _____

2. What words did Elisha repeat to all the others who also tried to stop him from staying with Elijah to the very end?

   _____

   _____

   _____

3. What did Elisha do as soon as Elijah was gone?

   _____

   _____

_____

4. Regarding his request of Elijah, do you think Elisha was testing (a) himself, (b) God, or (c) other?

_____

_____

_____

5. What does all this suggest to you about Elisha's relationship with the Lord?

_____

_____

_____

6. What does all of this say to you about Elisha's own sense of worth—that is, his self-image?

_____

_____

_____

7. What does all of this suggest about your own self-image? Should we be as persistent, determined, and convinced (but not falsely proud) of our merit as Elisha was?

_____

_____

_____

Another example of a good self-image, owned by a man who definitely had a close relationship with Jesus, is His beloved friend John. Note that, in all of these

Scriptures, the person indicated by the phrases in italics is the same person who authored the book.

When Jesus therefore saw His mother, and the disciple *whom He loved* standing by, He said to His mother, "Woman, behold your son!" (John 19:26 NKJV)

Then she ran and came to Simon Peter, and to the other disciple, *whom Jesus loved*, and said to them, "They have taken away the Lord out of the tomb, and we do not know where they have laid Him" (John 20:2 NKJV).

Therefore that disciple *whom Jesus loved* said to Peter, "It is the Lord!" Now when Simon Peter heard that it was the Lord, he put on his outer garment (for he had removed it), and plunged into the sea (John 21:7 NKJV).

Then Peter, turning around, saw the disciple *whom Jesus loved* following, who also had leaned on His breast at the supper, and said, "Lord, who is the one who betrays You?" (John 21:20, NKJV)

Enjoy the personality of the apostle John, and note what a healthy self-image he had.

BENEFITS 7 AND 8: WHOLE-PERSON PROSPERITY, GOOD HEALTH, AND A LONG LIFE

Each of these two benefits of walking wisely with God can be illustrated by a number of biblical accounts. For example, the story of Solomon illustrates how willing God is to pour out material blessings on someone who purposely seeks His wisdom. God gave good health and long life to other characters of the Bible, including King Hezekiah, to whom God granted an extra fifteen years. (Is. 38:1–5 and other Scriptures). Unfortunately, despite God's gift to him, Hezekiah apparently did not seek God's wisdom at all times for he did a very unwise thing before his fifteen years were completed—more about that later.

Words to Remember . . .

And let the peace of God rule in your hearts, to which also you were called in one body; and be thankful. Let the word of Christ dwell in you richly in all wisdom, teaching and admonishing one another in psalms and hymns and spiritual songs, singing with grace in your hearts to the Lord. And whatever you do in word or deed, do all in the name of the Lord Jesus, giving thanks to God the Father through Him (Col. 3:15–17 NKJV).

CLOSING PRAYER . . .

Our Father, help us to seek Your face in wisdom, to worship You in wisdom, to walk with You in wisdom, to realize the special blessings of divine wisdom that we know You desire to bestow upon Your own. May we always be wise enough to trust You as the ultimate source of all true wisdom.

In Jesus' name, Amen.

CHAPTER FOUR

THE ESSENTIALS FOR WALKING IN WISDOM

So far in this workbook we have defined wisdom, looked at many examples, and talked about its only true source. We have considered the difference between earthly wisdom and Godly wisdom and noted some of the joys and benefits that true wisdom can bring into our lives.

However, it is one thing to speak of walking in wisdom with the Lord but another thing entirely to do so on a regular basis. Exactly what "makes up" or *constitutes* heavenly wisdom? How do we know whether we're tapping into it?

Consider the definition given to us by Christ Himself in Matthew 11:19: "But wisdom is justified by her children" (NKJV).

In other words, wisdom is not just an abstract concept defined by whoever happens to be speaking. This is especially true of the wisdom of God. In the same way that our overall behavior (what Christ's own brother, James, called our "works") tends to indicate whether our hearts are truly given over to Him, some of the results we see in our lives also indicate *whether we are walking in His wisdom as well.*

God does not promise us a life without storms or thorns. He does promise us His presence, His help, and His rewards for our obedience in doing what He calls us to do.

The "children" of our "wisdom" are the results we see or in our lives. Perhaps Paul had this in mind when he said

> [We] . . . do not cease to pray for you, and to ask that you may be filled with the knowledge of His will in all *wisdom and spiritual understanding*; that you may walk worthy of the Lord, fully pleasing Him, being fruitful in every good work and increasing in the knowledge of God; strengthened with all might, according to His glorious power, for all patience and longsuffering with joy; giving thanks to the Father who has qualified us to be partakers of the inheritance of the saints in the light (Col. 1:9–12 NKJV, italics added).

In these four verses Paul gave the members of the church at Colossus at least seven benchmarks to help them know whether or not they were walking in wisdom with God. He begins with "filled with the knowledge of His will" and "walk(ing) worthy of the Lord." Can you find five more yardsticks that you might use to check your level of walking in wisdom with God?

_____

_____

_____

_____

_____

(BREAKOUT) WISDOM BENCHMARKS—FOR YOUR EYES ONLY!

This private exercise is intended for your own eyes only.

Review the benchmarks of godly wisdom identified by Paul in his letter to the Colossians. Now, consider how many are evident in your own life. Write a letter to God detailing which ones you feel are part of your life right now and which ones you are not seeing at this moment. What will you do? Can you pray *specifically* that God would help you add each one to the list of your own "children of godly wisdom"?

_____

_____

_____

_____

_____

_____

_____

Again, the question returns: How do we *get* wisdom in the first place? Walking in God's wisdom requires us to do at least seven fundamental things. Let's look at each of these *Seven Essentials* to see if we can make each one come alive.

ESSENTIAL 1: HAVE STRONG DETERMINATION TO WALK WISELY

As with all the other blessings of God, you don't get His wisdom accidentally. You have to want it, and you then have to purposely look for it.

The table below illustrates this point by listing several verses from the Bible's Old Testament "Wisdom Literature" (see the "What Is the Wisdom Literature?" article in this section). One or two of these might be familiar, but unless you study Proverbs and Ecclesiastes quite a bit, you might not recognize them. Nonetheless, each one conveys a concept that reinforces the idea that God's wisdom does not randomly fall on us; we get it by going after it.

Read each verse carefully. Then, underline the action words or phrases in each Scripture. These phrases *tell you what you need to do regarding wisdom*. Then, in the column on the right, list those same *action words or phrases* so they'll be easier to compare. The first entry is completed to give you the idea. In one or two cases these verses teach by "invoking a negative," meaning that they either tell you what *not* to do or indicate that others have failed in efforts to do so. However, the "action of the effort"—either doing or avoiding—was still valid and right.

SCRIPTURE	ACTION WORDS
Wisdom is the principal thing; Therefore get wisdom. And in all your getting, get understanding (Prov. 4:7 NKJV).	Get
A scoffer seeks wisdom and does not find it, But knowledge is easy to him who understands (Prov. 14:6 NKJV).	
Through wisdom a house is built, And by understanding it is established . . . (Prov. 24:3 NKJV).	
So shall the knowledge of wisdom be to your soul; If you have found it, there is a prospect, And your hope will not be cut off (Prov. 24:14 NKJV).	
And I set my heart to seek and search out by wisdom concerning all that is done under heaven; this burdensome task God has given to the sons of man, by which they may be exercised (Eccl. 1:13 NKJV).	
And I set my heart to know wisdom and to know madness and folly. I perceived that this also is grasping for the wind (Eccl. 1:17 NKJV).	

SCRIPTURE	ACTION WORDS
I applied my heart to know, To search and seek out wisdom and the reason of things, To know the wickedness of folly, Even of foolishness and madness (Eccl. 7:25 NKJV).	
Whatever your hand finds to do, do it with your might; for there is no work or device or knowledge or wisdom in the grave where you are going (Eccl. 9:10 NKJV).	
If the ax is dull, And one does not sharpen the edge, Then he must use more strength; But wisdom brings success (Eccl. 10:10 NKJV).	

Now that you've recognized the action words and phrases in the Scriptures, write a brief summary about what message you received. What do you clearly need to do to acquire Godly wisdom for yourself?

_____

_____

_____

_____

_____

_____

_____

(BREAKOUT) WHAT IS WISDOM LITERATURE?

The term wisdom literature is often applied to the Old Testament Books of Job, Proverbs, Ecclesiastes, and sometimes to the Song of Songs (Song of Solomon) as well. Wisdom literature can also include many of the Psalms, the teachings of Jesus, and some of the Book of James. All wisdom literature is somewhat different from most of the other biblical books in the following general ways:

FIRST, wisdom literature focuses on everyday life and speaks most often of how to live well in harmony with God (see #4).

SECOND, wisdom literature does not deal with "revealed truth" that comes directly from God. There will be no "Thus saith the Lord . . ." statements in it.

THIRD, wisdom literature does not claim to derive its authority directly from God, as do the words of Moses, the prophets, and the New Testament authors. Tradition and human observation play an active role.

FOURTH, wisdom literature assumes a great deal of reverence and commitment to God.

ESSENTIAL 2: PRAY FOR WISDOM

We have already mentioned King Solomon a number of times in this workbook. Now, rather than discussing Solomon by himself, let's do a comparison-and-contrast exercise. Let's look at the difference between what happened to Solomon, as a direct result of his well-known prayer for wisdom, and what happened to another king, who lived more or less at the same time and who obviously did *not* pray the same prayer—or anything remotely similar!

Begin with the words of Solomon, and the Lord's response, from 1 Kings 3:7–14:

"Now, O LORD my God, You have made Your servant king instead of my father David, but I am a little child; I do not know how to go out or come in. And Your servant is in the midst of Your people whom You have chosen, a great people, too numerous to be numbered or counted. Therefore give to Your servant an understanding heart to judge Your people, that I may discern between good and evil. For who is able to judge this great people of Yours?"

The speech pleased the LORD, that Solomon had asked this thing. Then God said to him: "Because you have asked this thing, and have not asked long life for yourself, nor have asked riches for yourself, nor have asked the life of your enemies, but have asked for yourself understanding to discern justice, behold, I have done according to your words; see, I have given you a wise and understanding heart, so that there has not been anyone like you before you, nor shall any like you arise after you. And I have also given you what you have not asked: both riches and honor, so that there shall not be anyone like you among the kings all your days. So if you walk in My ways, to keep My statutes and My commandments, as your father David walked, then I will lengthen your days" (NKJV).

Read the words of the Lord, as given to Ezekiel (28:1–10), fill in the blanks below, and then answer the questions that follow:

The word of the LORD came to me again, saying, "Son of man, say to the prince of Tyre, "Thus says the Lord GOD:

"Because your heart is _____ _____, And you say, "I am a god, I sit in the seat of gods, In the midst of the seas,' Yet you are a man, and not a god, Though you set your heart as the heart of a god.

(Behold, you are wiser than Daniel! There is no secret that can be hidden from you! With your wisdom and your _____ You have gained riches for yourself, And gathered gold and silver into your treasuries; By your great wisdom in trade you have _____ your riches, And your heart is lifted up because of your riches),"

"Therefore thus says the Lord GOD:

Because you have set your heart as the heart of a god, Behold, therefore, I will bring strangers against you, The most _____ of the nations; And they shall draw their swords against the beauty of your wisdom, And _____ your splendor. They shall throw you down into the Pit, And you shall die the death of the slain In the midst of the seas. "Will you still say before him who slays you, "I am a god'? But you shall be a man, and not a god, In the hand of him who slays you. You shall die the death of the uncircumcised By the hand of _____; For I have spoken," says the Lord GOD'" (NKJV).

1. First, to whom did Solomon and the King of Tyre (here called a "prince"—Tyre was a coastal city in what was known as Phoenicia in Solomon's day) give credit for their success in life?

   _____

   _____

   _____

2. Describe each man's relationship to God: Was it close? Distant? Non-existent?

   _____

   _____

   _____

3. What was the connection between each man's relationship to God and the way God dealt with him? Was it direct or indirect? (Note: While it's true that Solomon turned away from God in his later years, for this discussion consider only his early years when he remained true.)

   _____

   _____

   _____

4. What is the obvious deduction you can make about your own walk in wisdom with God?

_____

_____

_____

❋ (BREAKOUT) STRAIGHT FROM THE BOOK . . .

Those who have the Holy Spirit resident in their spirits do not automatically make wise choices and engage in wise actions. Furthermore, it is one thing to know what to do and another thing to do it. We must consciously and intentionally ask the Holy Spirit to guide us into wisdom and give us the courage to walk in it.

ESSENTIAL 3: MEDITATE ON GOD'S WORD

Look up each of these Scriptures and fill in the blanks. Then answer the questions below.

JOSHUA 1:8

This Book of the Law shall not depart from your mouth, but you shall _____ in it day and night, that you may observe to do according to all that is written in it. For then you will make your way prosperous, and then you will have good success (NKJV).

PSALM 63:6

When I remember You on my bed, I _____ on You in the night watches (NKJV).

PSALM 77:6

I call to remembrance my song in the night; I _____ within my heart, And my spirit makes diligent search (NKJV).

PSALM 77:12

I will also _____ on all Your work, And talk of Your deeds (NKJV).

PSALM 119:15

I will _____ on Your precepts, And contemplate Your ways (NKJV).

PSALM 119:27

Make me understand the way of Your precepts; So shall I _____ on Your wonderful works (NKJV).

PSALM 119:48

My hands also I will lift up to Your commandments, Which I love, And I will _____ on Your statutes (NKJV).

PSALM 119:78

Let the proud be ashamed, For they treated me wrongfully with falsehood; But I will _____ on Your precepts (NKJV).

PSALM 119:148

My eyes are awake through the night watches, That I may _____ on Your word (NKJV).

PSALM 143:5

I remember the days of old; I _____ on all Your works; I muse on the work of Your hands (NKJV).

PSALM 145:5

I will _____ on the glorious splendor of Your majesty, And on Your wondrous works (NKJV).

MALACHI 3:16

Then those who feared the LORD spoke to one another, And the LORD listened and heard them; So a book of remembrance was written before Him For those who fear the LORD And who _____ on His name (NKJV).

PHILIPPIANS 4:8

Finally, brethren, whatever things are true, whatever things are noble, whatever things are just, whatever things are pure, whatever things are lovely, whatever things are of good report, if there is any virtue and if there is anything praiseworthy—_____on these things (NKJV).

1 TIMOTHY 4:15

_____ on these things; give yourself entirely to them, that your progress may be evident to all (NKJV).

Most of these Scriptures were from Psalms written by David, one of the premier meditators of the Bible. As you undoubtedly discovered very quickly, the missing word in each case is "meditate." Repetition tends to solidify understanding.

1. Go back through these Scriptures and create a list of all the things we are told to meditate on.

   _____ _____ _____

   _____ _____ _____

   _____ _____ _____

   _____ _____ _____

   _____ _____ _____

   _____ _____ _____

   _____ _____ _____

2. How many did you find?

_____

_____

_____

3. More important, on how many of these things do you already meditate on a regular basis?

_____

_____

_____

4. What value do you see in meditating daily on the items in your list?

_____

_____

_____

Let's conclude this section by considering Genesis 24:63: "And Isaac went out to meditate in the field in the evening; and he lifted his eyes and looked, and there, the camels were coming" (NKJV).

In case you have not read the entire story of Isaac and Rebekah recently, to know what's happening here, Isaac's servant is returning from his trip back to the land of Abraham's birth (Abraham is Isaac's father), where he found Rebekah among Abraham's own people and asked her to return with him to marry Isaac. The camels that Isaac sees when he "lifts up his eyes" and looks are the ones bringing him his future bride.

Isaac was not yet married in this passage. He might not have been a youth as we define that word today, but he was certainly in the prime of his physical life, ready for the responsibilities of supporting a wife and rearing a family. What does he do, after finishing his work in the evening, in an act that is described so casually it sounds as though it was an ordinary occurrence for him?

He goes out to the field to meditate. He wasn't old, he didn't work as a research scholar in a university, and he didn't have a degree in theology. He was an ordinary man doing what ordinary people should do.

He was meditating.

ESSENTIAL 4: ACTIVELY OBEY AND APPLY GOD'S WORD

The New Testament contains hundreds of quotations from the Old. Experts do not agree on precisely how many, for some involve exact words, some alter the words slightly while retaining the meaning, and others refer to concepts and ideas but do not re-state the original.

What matters is the message, and the message to be gleaned from all this is that—like the first-century authors of the New Testament—we should be as familiar as possible with God's Word. After all, He is the ultimate source of wisdom, but His Word is the means by which *He Himself chose to deliver His wisdom to us on a daily basis*!

To become familiar with just a few examples in which the Scriptures literally *reinforce themselves*, work through the following list. Begin by looking up the New Testament scripture in the first column and then compare that with the Old Testament scripture in the second column, to which the first one refers. Then, in the third column, quote the *exact words that are repeated*, or indicate the *subject* both Scriptures discuss.

NEW TESTAMENT	OLD TESTAMENT	SUBJECT
1. Luke 4:4	Deut. 8:3	
2. Matt. 4:6	Ps. 91:11, 12	
3. Matt. 4:7	Deut. 6:16	

NEW TESTAMENT	OLD TESTAMENT	SUBJECT
4. Luke 4:9	Deut. 6:13	
5. Luke 19:46	Jer. 7:11	
6. John 6:31	Ex. 16:4; Ps. 78:24	
7. Acts 23:5	Ex. 22:28	
8. Rom. 1:17	Hab. 2:4	
9. Rom. 8:36	Ps. 44:22	
10. Rom. 12:19	Deut. 32:35	
11. Rom. 14:11	Is. 45:23	
12. 1 Cor. 1:19	Is. 29:14	
13. 1 Cor. 3:19	Job 5:13	
14. 1 Cor. 9:9	Deut 25:4	

15. 1 Pet. 1:16 Lev. 11:44, 45

____________________ ____________________ ____________________

If you find this exercise interesting and helpful, you can pursue it further by using a Bible concordance. Bible software or a Bible search engine on the Internet can also be very useful.

Either way, you will be amazed at how much the Bible reinforces and amplifies itself!

(Breakout) Who Quoted Scripture in the Bible?

The *New King James Version* (NKJV) of the Bible lists seventy-eight instances of the words *it is written*, referring to other scriptural quotations. Seventeen of these occur in the Old Testament. Of the remainder, sixteen involve references made by Christ Himself, a few of which are duplicates from the Books of Matthew and Luke.

Another *it is written* comes from the devil, quoting Scripture while tempting Christ, to which Christ's direct response is a more appropriate quotation. Meanwhile, the apostle Paul quotes Old Testament Scriptures once in the Book of Acts and twenty-nine additional times in his letters. Peter uses the expression only once, as does the writer of Hebrews.

Essential 5: Be Sensitive to the Prompting of the Holy Spirit

Look up the following verses, fill in the blanks, and then answer the questions.

Romans 5:5

Now hope does not disappoint, because the love of God has been poured out in our hearts by the ____________ ____________ who was given to us (NKJV).

1 CORINTHIANS 6:19

Or do you not know that your body is the temple of the _____ _____ who is in you, whom you have from God, and you are not your own? (NKJV)

2 CORINTHIANS 13:14

The grace of the Lord Jesus Christ, and the love of God, and the communion of the _____ _____ be with you all (NKJV).

2 TIMOTHY 1:14

That good thing which was committed to you, keep by the _____ _____ who dwells in us (NKJV).

HEBREWS 3:7

Therefore, as the _____ _____ says: "Today, if you will hear His voice . . . (NKJV).

HEBREWS 10:14

But the _____ _____ also witnesses to us . . . (NKJV).

1. What is the general theme, or "thrust," of the verses above?

   _____

   _____

   _____

   _____

   _____

2. Even though a "time and circumstances" element is not mentioned, when and under what conditions would you say the Holy Spirit is "on duty" within us?

   _____

_____

_____

The Bible tells us over and over that, at the moment we accept salvation as offered by God, the Holy Spirit comes and lives within us. The verses above are just a few of those that mention how the Holy Spirit functions—as a comforter, as a constant reminder of God's love, as a source of strength, and as a prompter and a leader. The Holy Spirit also convicts us of sin and helps guide us into corrective action whenever we have been fooled by the tricks of the devil.

In addition, the Holy Spirit also calls us into the service of God. One of the most endearing passages in the Old Testament involves exactly that.[2] Turn to First Samuel 3:3–10, fill in the blanks, and answer the questions.

> . . . and before the lamp of God went out in the tabernacle of the LORD where the ark of God was, and while Samuel was _____ _____, that the LORD called Samuel. And he answered, "Here I am!" So he ran to Eli and said, "Here I am, for you called me."
>
> And he said, "I did not call; _____ down again." And he went and lay down.
>
> Then the LORD _____ yet again, "Samuel!"
>
> So Samuel _____ and went to Eli, and said, "Here I am, for you called me." He answered, "I did not call, my son; lie down again." (Now Samuel did not yet know the LORD, nor was the word of the LORD yet revealed to him.)
>
> And the LORD _____ Samuel again the third time. So he arose and went to Eli, and said, "Here I am, for you did call me."
>
> Then Eli perceived that the LORD had called the boy. Therefore Eli said to Samuel, "Go, lie down; and it shall be, if He calls you, that you must say, 'Speak, LORD, for Your servant hears.'" So Samuel went and lay down in his place.

Now the LORD came and stood and _____ as at other times, "Samuel! Samuel!"

And Samuel answered, "Speak, for Your servant hears."

1. Who was calling Samuel?

_____

_____

_____

2. Who did Samuel *think* was calling him?

_____

_____

_____

3. Why did Samuel not know better?

_____

_____

_____

4. Was Eli a good teacher for Samuel? Why or why not?

_____

_____

_____

5. Based on verse 10 above (the final portion), do you think God was pleased with Samuel? Why, or why not?

_____

❉ (BREAKOUT) STRAIGHT FROM THE BOOK . . .

You may be saying, "Well, this sounds like intuition." I encourage you to change your vocabulary. If you are a believer in Christ Jesus, you have the Holy Spirit living inside you, and He desires to lead you step-by-step into the fullness of God's plan and provision for you. Intuition for the believer has a name: Holy Spirit.

ESSENTIAL 6: OBSERVE GOD'S WORK

One of the most profound and yet condemnatory verses in the Bible is Romans 1:20—*profound* because it teaches something we should all know yet which we seldom acknowledge; *condemnatory* because—as the verse itself says—it leaves those who would deny God's sovereignty utterly "without excuse." The text:

> For since the creation of the world His invisible attributes are clearly seen, being understood by the things that are made, even His eternal power and Godhead, so that they are without excuse . . . (Rom. 1:20 NKJV).

To reinforce the message above, look up the following verses and fill in the blanks.

The heavens declare the glory of God; And the _____ shows His handiwork (Ps. 19:1 NKJV).

Let the heavens declare His _____, For God Himself is Judge (Ps. 50:6 NKJV).

The heavens declare His righteousness, And all the _____ see His glory (Ps. 97:6 NKJV).

Indeed, one of the ironies of modern times is the extent to which God's creation proves itself more and more to be designed and built by a God with intellect and abilities far beyond anything remotely human or temporal. Every time man thinks he has built a microscope powerful enough to reveal the tiniest particles of creation, he finds a whole new universe in miniature. Every time man builds a telescope powerful enough to see to the outer edge of the universe, he discovers still more, beyond what he once thought was the absolute end of it all.

A wise man observes the beauty and intricacy of God's work—and worships Him all the more.

⚜ (BREAKOUT) STRAIGHT FROM THE BOOK . . .

Jesus did not tell His followers to study the writings of some famous scholar in order to understand God's message—He said simply, "Look around you. Look at the birds and the flowers! The world is filled with lessons about God's provision and faithfulness."

ESSENTIAL 7: ASSOCIATE WITH AND LEARN FROM WISE PEOPLE

The words "gathered together" appear a number of times in the New Testament, almost always referring to the people of God "gathering together" to pray, worship, and hear the good news of salvation. For example, refer to Matthew 13:2, 18:20; Luke 24:33; Acts 12:12, 14:27, 14:30, 20:8; 1 Corinthians 5:4. All these Scriptures repeat the message: The children of God are like a family of scholars that gathers together, studies His Word, praises His name, and speaks of who He is.

The Christians of the New Testament continued the traditions of the children of Israel begun back in the wilderness between Egypt and Canaan, and even before that. There's a good reason.

God designed us to associate together, to be lonely *without* each other even as He was lonely without man. More to the point, He designed us to *learn* from each other, to understand His wisdom better even as we understood each other—and to walk accordingly.

Words to Remember . . .

To God our Savior, Who alone is wise, Be glory and majesty, Dominion and power, Both now and forever (Jude 1:25 NKJV).

Closing Prayer . . .

Our Father, we pray that we might learn how *to walk in wisdom with You—not to have You* do it for us *but to identify, study, perfect, and cherish on our own those things that will help make us wise. May our hearts and minds be open to Your eternal, all-encompassing wisdom, wherever found in all its forms.*

In Jesus' name, Amen.

CHAPTER FIVE

WISDOM FOR CONFRONTING TEMPTATION

Recently I heard a story told by a man who traveled extensively on business. This particular gentleman had been dealing with a weakness for pornography, going back a number of years. Sadly, hundreds and perhaps thousands of modern hotels and motels now offer x-rated television channels, x-rated rental movies, and video machines that will also play anything the user might bring along. More than once this man had been tempted; more than once he'd given in.

What made his situation even more difficult was the loneliness of the road. Every night a new hotel; every night a new room; every night a new temptation; and every night he was alone.

Finally he asked the Lord to give him the strength to wipe out an addiction that he had tried repeatedly to starve to death but never could. The Lord helped him, but not in the way that he expected. The man felt very clearly that, rather than removing his weakness, God sent him to the same verse in Genesis that we looked at earlier in chapter three of this study guide.

In this case the Lord spoke directly to Cain just before Cain made his decision to murder his brother, and said:

> But if you do not do what is right, sin is _____ at your door;
> it desires to have you, but you must master it" (Gen. 4:7 NKJV).

We all know that Cain lost his battle with sin in a big way, but this man did not. From that day forward, whenever he arrived at a new hotel he immediately called the front desk and asked them to remove his television set and all the ads for movie rentals and TV channels. "Demanded" might be a better word, for this is really what he did. Many times they thought he was crazy; more than once they told him to just "Ignore it!" if he didn't want to use it. However, he insisted, and each time he got his way. Eventually he even learned how to specify his requirements in advance, and after a time, like a waiter who serves you the same sandwich five times a week, the places he frequented became proactive themselves and began asking if he wanted his "usual" accommodations.

It took a lot of determination, but by taking charge, physically changing his environment, and substituting healthful activities instead (such as reading his Bible), he gradually lost the recurring urge to give in to Satan's temptations. After all, said the man, who but *he himself* had the right to determine what would appear before his eyes, on his own time, in his own room?

Who, indeed?

✿ (Breakout) Straight from the Book . . .

Temptation is an enticement of our natural, God-given desires to take them beyond God-given limits or boundaries.

THE WORLD, THE FLESH, AND THE DEVIL

Probably you have heard "the world, the flesh, and the devil" referring to the traditional *sources* of temptation. What do those words mean in real life?

Consider the following scenarios. Then, for each one indicate whether the temptation it describes come from **W** (for "world"), **F** (for "flesh"), or **D** (for "devil"). Then we'll talk about your answers . . .

1. You're at home for the evening. You're on a diet to lose twenty pounds. The doctor says you'll have serious problems if you don't stick with it, but there's this gorgeous box of candy sitting on the shelf . . .

   _____

2. You're conducting an inventory for the store you work for. You're alone in the back room when you find an old billfold containing $487 lying behind some boxes. You've seen that billfold before—it belonged to a fellow who left the company a long time ago. And there's probably no way to find him again . . .

   _____

3. You're in an airplane when you notice a folded $20 bill under the seat ahead of you. It probably hasn't been there long; too visible; too many people would have seen it. Maybe it fell out of the purse of the lady who's sitting there now . . .

   _____

4. You're at a company retreat, 1,500 miles from home, and your young assistant comes up to you after the last meeting of the evening, looking great. You know she's had an eye on you; there's an all-night café just down the street. Would you like some coffee—or a glass of wine—before you turn in for the night?

   _____

5. You're filling out a job application. You really need this one—you've been out of work ever since the markets went south, six months ago. You deserve it! They want someone with a Master's Degree, but you had to drop out three months before you actually got yours. Hey—who ever checks these things, anyway?

   _____

6. You're in a strange city on business, and you have an afternoon to kill. There's an incredible antique store just down the block, begging to be explored. Another block over there's a whole row of sex shops and x-rated movie theaters. No one knows you, and no one's keeping score . . .

   _____

7. Your car insurance just expired, and you've selected a new policy. It won't take effect for another week, after your payment arrives, but it was icy and you slid into a tree today! Your car is drivable, and you didn't file a police report. So you could just report all this as "new" to your insurance company in a month or two . . .

   _____

8. You handed the clerk a $10 bill, and she gave you change for $20. She just closed her drawer and turned to her next customer . . .

   _____

9. You're in a restaurant, and the bill comes. You've had a lovely dinner with your family, including several terrific desserts that everyone shared, but the bill doesn't list any of them . . .

   _____

How you responded to these scenarios is not really the point of this exercise. Some of them could clearly be answered in more than one way—is it the world, your flesh, or the devil who's tempting you, for example, to cheat on your husband or wife? Could it be all three? The more important exercise is to develop defenses against temptations of these kinds.

THREE BIBLICAL TEMPTATIONS

Let's consider three examples of temptation from the Bible. The events that led up to at least two of these three examples are well-known and often talked about in Sunday school classes, but in the portions of the stories I have included below we do not see simple cases of clear-cut, action-reaction, right-wrong activities. All three examples involved men who were (1) used mightily by God, (2) given great favor by God, or (3) participated in great things with God's blessings. Yet each story also tells of someone who yielded to temptation of one kind of another—of the *world*, of the *flesh*, or of the *devil*—and made a mistake he should not have made.

❖ (BREAKOUT) STRAIGHT FROM THE BOOK . . .

All of us are responsible for our own behavior and choices. We cannot avoid temptation, but we can control our response to temptation. If we yield to a temptation, we can choose our next response. Is your first reaction after you have yielded to a temptation to blame God, someone else, or a circumstance?

Let me add one or two additional words of explanation before you read these stories.

FIRST, each story might benefit from a short introduction in order to set the scene and review one or two important details. I have provided that in the italicized paragraph that precedes each one.

SECOND, all the questions for all three stories are given to you in advance so you can be thinking about them as you read. The stories are numbered for reference—but first, the questions:

1. In each of these stories, did anyone commit any obvious sins or make any serious mistakes?

_____

_____

_____

2. If so, who were they, and what were those sins or mistakes?

_____

_____

_____

_____

3. In each case, what temptations did they yield to?

_____

_____

_____

_____

4. List each of those temptations below, and indicate whether they came from the *world*, the *flesh*, or the *devil*.

_____

_____

_____

_____

_____

_____

Now, the stories . . .

1. **From the story of Joshua AFTER he won the Battle of Jericho . . .**

(God instructed Joshua and his men to use several unorthodox techniques, but they did as He commanded and were victorious in the famous battle of Jericho. After the

walls fell down and the Israelites won the battle, one of Joshua's men secretly disobeyed one of God's instructions about how they were to deal with the spoils. Joshua's army then lost a battle against the men of Ai, which they should have won easily. Joshua tore his clothes and asked God what was wrong. God responded by identifying Achan, the culprit, who was eventually stoned and burned, along with his family, after he revealed the following . . .)

JOSHUA 7:19–21

So Joshua said to Achan, "My son, I beg you, give glory to the LORD God of Israel, and make confession to Him, and tell me now what you have done; do not hide it from me."

And Achan answered Joshua and said, "Indeed I have sinned against the LORD God of Israel, and this is what I have done: When I saw among the spoils a beautiful Babylonian garment, two hundred shekels of silver, and a wedge of gold weighing fifty shekels, I coveted them and took them. And there they are, hidden in the earth in the midst of my tent, with the silver under it" (NKJV).

✳ (BREAKOUT) STRAIGHT FROM THE BOOK . . .

Not every person can be tempted by everything, and not all people are tempted by the same things. Each one has a propensity toward a certain temptation. Temptations also may change as a person moves through the various stages of life. What tempts a person when he is a teenager may not be what tempts him when he is fifty years old.

2. **From the story of Gideon AFTER the Battle . . .**

(In the time when Israel was ruled by judges, before they anointed their first king, Gideon was an ordinary farmer who was called by the Lord to save Israel from the Midianites. God gave him an army, then cut it from several thousand men to just 300,

in a series of fascinating "elimination rounds." God gave Gideon and his 300 men a great victory; this part of the story resumes just after the battle is over.)

JUDGES 8:22–27

Then the men of Israel said to Gideon, "Rule over us, both you and your son, and your grandson also; for you have delivered us from the hand of Midian."

But Gideon said to them, "I will not rule over you, nor shall my son rule over you; the LORD shall rule over you." Then Gideon said to them, "I would like to make a request of you, that each of you would give me the earrings from his plunder." For they had golden earrings, because they were Ishmaelites.

So they answered, "We will gladly give them." And they spread out a garment, and each man threw into it the earrings from his plunder. Now the weight of the gold earrings that he requested was one thousand seven hundred shekels of gold, besides the crescent ornaments, pendants, and purple robes which were on the kings of Midian, and besides the chains that were around their camels' necks. Then Gideon made it into an ephod and set it up in his city, Ophrah. And all Israel played the harlot with it there. *It became a snare to Gideon and to his house* (NKJV, italics added).

3. **From the story of Hezekiah AFTER he got those Extra Years . . .**

(Hezekiah, king of Israel, followed the Lord and saw the Lord give His people some great military victories. Later on, when Hezekiah lay dying, he even asked God to give him a longer life and got fifteen more years. However, he didn't use all that additional time wisely . . .)

2 KINGS 20:12–19

At that time Berodach-Baladan the son of Baladan, king of Babylon, sent letters and a present to Hezekiah, for he heard that Hezekiah had been sick. And Hezekiah was attentive to them, and showed them all the house of his treasures—the silver and gold, the spices and precious ointment, and all his armory—all that was found among his treasures. There was nothing in his house or in all his dominion that Hezekiah did not show them.

Then Isaiah the prophet went to King Hezekiah, and said to him, "What did these men say, and from where did they come to you?"

So Hezekiah said, "They came from a far country, from Babylon."

And he said, "What have they seen in your house?"

So Hezekiah answered, "They have seen all that is in my house; there is nothing among my treasures that I have not shown them."

Then Isaiah said to Hezekiah, "Hear the word of the LORD: "Behold, the days are coming when all that is in your house, and what your fathers have accumulated until this day, shall be carried to Babylon; nothing shall be left,' says the LORD. "And they shall take away some of your sons who will descend from you, whom you will beget; and they shall be eunuchs in the palace of the king of Babylon.'"

So Hezekiah said to Isaiah, "The word of the LORD which you have spoken is good!" For he said, "Will there not be peace and truth at least in my days?" (NKJV)

(BREAKOUT) HEY, MAN—IT DIDN'T HAPPEN ON MY WATCH!

Look at the final words of Hezekiah in story #3, taken from the Book of Second Kings. Hezekiah has just finished showing everything he owns to the son of the king of Babylon, including not only his gold and his jewels but all the weapons in his armory as well.

Then, when Isaiah rebukes him, he agrees with Isaiah and adds the following comment: "Will there not be peace and truth at least in my days?"

What does this tell us about the character of Hezekiah? If you believe this shows some negative traits, what do you think he should have said instead?

_____

_____

_____

_____

_____

Now, let's talk for a moment about larger comments with respect to temptation and how we can resist it and continue to walk in wisdom with God. Then we'll return to the three stories.

BUILDING A DEFENSE AGAINST TEMPTATION

Many football coaches agree that "The best defense is a good offense," but the opposite is also true—the best offense can be a good defense. Let's talk about ways to defend yourself against temptation, and then let's tie this discussion back into everything we've said so far.

✳ (BREAKOUT) STRAIGHT FROM THE BOOK . . .

God will never entice a person to act in a way that is contrary to His commandments. He does not have any association with sin, and He certainly does not entice His people to sin and suffer sin's consequences.

Studying the table below, list things you can do to build your defense against temptation, together with *very short* explanations of each one. Refer to the book

WISDOM FOR CONFRONTING TEMPTATION

Walking Wisely for more detailed discussions of these actions. In *all* cases, remember that you might benefit greatly by getting additional, *godly* counsel to help you implement any of these actions.

ACTION	EXPLANATION
1. Resolve to obey God.	Make the commitment. Then, visualize yourself saying "No!" to temptations. Create *new* mental tapes and discard the old.
2. Identify your personal areas of frequent temptation.	Do a personal inventory. It would not hurt to make a list. *Be honest* with yourself.
3. Address the needs that make you vulnerable.	Figure out what hidden need(s) the temptations in your life address. Then find other good, right, and more godly ways to deal with those needs.
4. Short-Circuit the thought process of temptation.	Learn to recognize the thoughts that lead to temptation and consciously reject them.
5. Confront the element of deception.	Identify the consequences of any ungodly temptation and ask yourself if you are prepared to lose more than you will gain.
6. Put on the whole armor of God.	Do this every morning, by consciously praying, "Lord, I put on (name of item) to (identify the way this item will protect you – *see main text*).
7. Maintain a big-picture focus; use HALT acronym.	Anticipate trouble points; do not knowingly take "first steps." Never allow yourself to become too Hungry, Angry, Lonely, or Tired.
8. Build accountability into your life.	Find a mentor, counselor, or close friend. Do a "temptations" inventory together; stay in touch; call as needed.
9. Cry out to God for help.	Call on God! He will *NOT* ask you to endure more than you are able.

Now let's reconsider our three biblical excerpts. In the first column in the table below, you will see the name of the person who yielded to temptation in each of those excerpts. Then, the next nine columns correspond to the actions you can take to defend yourself, in a preemptive fashion, against temptation.

To complete the first three lines in the table, indicate by adding a check mark whether you believe the person in question actually took the action that corresponds to the suggested actions in the table above. Then, in the last column, enter the total number of checkmarks.

PERSON	TEMPTATION OR SIN	1	2	3	4	5	6	7	8	9	TOTAL
Achan											
Gideon											
Hezekiah											

After you have finished this exercise, you can then use the table in a number of ways. Consider the following possibilities:

1. If you are part of a study group, take suggestions and add the names of any number of additional biblical characters, referenced to specific temptations and/or sins, then rate them accordingly to see how well they defended themselves.

2. Do exactly the same for yourself with respect to each of the temptations you have identified in your own life. This action will require you to take a serious inventory and fill out a blank table, but the scores you will then derive can be immensely helpful. They will help you clearly identify the areas in your

life in which you are most vulnerable—areas you need to start working on immediately.

May God help you walk wisely with Him and to be honest, diligent, and totally committed to doing this very necessary work of building your godly defenses against temptation.

(BREAKOUT) A LETTER TO GOD

Recall everything we've said thus far about the "knowledge versus wisdom" dynamic—clearly the two are not the same. Just as clearly, acquiring the first does not automatically lead to acquiring the second—certainly not if our goal is godly rather than worldly wisdom.

What large "body of knowledge" have you acquired in your own life? Has it led to wisdom? Have you turned it over to God for *His* use? How would you do that? What might His response be if you did?

If you haven't turned it over, write a "Letter to God" explaining why. If you have, write a letter to God exploring the ways that He has blessed you as a result.

_____

_____

_____

_____

_____

_____

_____

_____

WORDS TO REMEMBER . . .

Blessed is the man
>Who walks not in the counsel of the ungodly,
>Nor stands in the path of sinners,
>Nor sits in the seat of the scornful;
>But his delight is in the law of the LORD,
>And in His law he meditates day and night.
>He shall be like a tree
>Planted by the rivers of water,
>That brings forth its fruit in its season,
>Whose leaf also shall not wither;
>And whatever he does shall prosper (Ps. 1:1–3 NKJV).

CLOSING PRAYER . . .

Our Father, we pray for Your divine guidance in learning not only to resist but to utterly prevent needless temptation. May we walk with You in wisdom, and may we learn to identify, eliminate, avoid, and always to resist those temptations that might otherwise cause us to stumble.

In Jesus' name, Amen.

(BREAKOUT) THE FINISHING TOUCH

By the time Satan had finished with him, Job literally had nothing beyond his unshakable belief that God's wisdom, God's judgment, and God's purposes were *best* for him even though he didn't understand them. Therefore, *even though the pain they brought him caused him tears of anguish,* he held fast in his loyalty and reverence to God—literally, his *fear of the Lord*!

In the spaces below, give examples of how hardship has helped you develop wisdom.

Based on what you've learned about true, godly wisdom, *what would you now do, or say, that you might not have done or said before?*

_____

_____

_____

_____

_____

_____

_____

_____

CHAPTER SIX

WISDOM IN CHOOSING FRIENDS AND BUSINESS ASSOCIATES

To introduce this chapter I tried to write a bit of poetry:

> *Wisdom comes in many forms,*
> *But only from one source.*
> *The source, of course, is God alone;*
> *The forms _____ _____ _____ _____*

and that's where the whole thing came to an end. Not, I might add, because I couldn't find anything to rhyme with "source," but because "bourse," "horse," "force," "remorse," and any number of other words do not quite complete the thought. So let me try it in prose.

As the title of the chapter tells us, forms of wisdom permeate making wise choices when we build friendships and align ourselves with business associates.

However, chapter seven *also* deals with how to make the same wise choices, but from an entirely different perspective.

To clarify, then, this chapter deals with things we should *not* do. The next chapter deals with things we *should* do, therefore explaining what might otherwise be thought of as "negativity" in this chapter. Wisdom consists of making the right choices, but it also consists of avoiding the wrong ones.

Let's first talk about avoiding wrong choices.

(Breakout) Straight from the Book . . .

Never assume that just because a person seeks you out, you are in close proximity to a person, or an acquaintanceship with a person seems to develop quickly, that God has sent this person to you. Ask Him!

People Who Should Not Be Your Friends

Each of the following Scriptures refers specifically to one kind of person who should not be your friend. Read each verse and then from the list that follows the last (sixth) entry, select the kind of person the Bible verse describes. Write the names in the spaces above their corresponding verses.

(Breakout) Proverbs and Wisdom Literature

In a previous chapter we learned that what is often called wisdom literature includes, primarily, the Books of Job, Proverbs, Ecclesiastes, and the Song of Solomon. Of these, all but Job were written (in whole or in part) by Solomon, the wisest man who ever lived. Obviously, they were not all written during the same time period in his life—Ecclesiastes is very different from Proverbs, and both of those are very different from his portion of Song of Solomon.

However, all the verses we have used in this chapter, to illustrate six examples of the kinds of people it would *not* be wise to associate with on a regular basis, come from Proverbs, which is by far the Bible's most overflowing treasure chest of wisdom "pearls."

On the other hand, Proverbs is often overlooked by many Christians who believe it has nothing new, or fresh, to offer compared to the wisdom of the world. In reality, a huge share of that worldly wisdom derives directly from Proverbs—not the other way around. It is often called "too simplistic" and even "too clever by half."

Don't you believe this unwise trap!

He who goes about as a talebearer reveals secrets; Therefore do not associate with one who flatters with his lips (Prov. 20:19 NKJV).

1. _____

Make no friendship with an angry man, And with a furious man do not go, Lest you learn his ways And set a snare for your soul (Prov. 22:24 NKJV).

2. _____

My son, fear the LORD and the king; Do not associate with those given to change; For their calamity will rise suddenly, And who knows the ruin those two can bring? (Prov. 24:21, 22 NKJV)

3. _____

Whoever keeps the law is a discerning son, But a companion of gluttons shames his father (Prov. 28:7 NKJV).

4. _____

Whoever loves wisdom makes his father rejoice, But a companion of harlots wastes his wealth (Prov. 29:3 NKJV).

5. _____

A wise son makes a father glad, But a foolish man despises his mother. Folly is joy to him who is destitute of discernment, But a man of understanding walks uprightly (Prov. 15:20, 21 NKJV).

6. _____

Fool   **Self-Indulgent**   **Rebellious**
Gossip   **Sexually Immoral**   **Quick-Tempered**

> ❖ (BREAKOUT) STRAIGHT FROM THE BOOK . . .
>
> The dearest treasure of your life—second only to your relationship with Jesus Christ—is a close friend. A genuine friend is a gift of God's mercy to you. However . . . God's foremost wisdom regarding your friendships and business associations is this: Be careful whom you choose.

Now let's build on what we've established. The Scriptures in the following table contain enough information about the person who's the main subject to tell you what kind of person he or she was. In fact, many of the selections are slightly longer than they absolutely have to be in order to give you the name of the character involved and the personal characteristic his or her actions tend to typify.

Your challenge is to choose the characteristics, from the previous list, that best describe each person. This list does *not* include all possible human personality characteristics, but for this exercise, please select only from that list (there will be some duplication). Then, consider the questions below the table.

SCRIPTURE	CHARACTER	CHARACTERISTIC(S)
Numbers 12:1–16	Miriam	
Matthew 7:26, 27	Foolish Builder	
1 Corinthians 5:1–5	Corinthian Christian	
Genesis 4:23	Lamech	
Luke 15:11–32	Prodigal Son	
1 Kings 11:3	King Solomon	
Judges 15:1–5	Samson	
2 Samuel 20:1, 2	Sheba	
Numbers 22:22–29	Balaam	
Luke 16:19	Rich Man	
2 Samuel 11:1–26	David	
Matthew 25:1–13	Foolish Virgins	
John 4:6–19	Woman at the Well	
Esther 5:9–14	Haman	
Luke 12:16–21	Rich Fool	

1. (Num. 12:1–16) Was Miriam the only person involved in gossiping about Moses? If not, why do you suppose she was the only one punished?

_____

_____

_____

2. How would you feel if Miriam and her brother Aaron were questioning your authority and your stewardship of the job God had called you to do?

_____

_____

_____

3. (Luke 12:16–21) What obvious possibility did the rich fool, who stored up several years' worth of food, overlook? (Hint: How certain could it be that his stored goods would still be there and still be usable when he wanted them?)

_____

_____

_____

4. How would you like having him for a friend? Would he be generous with his windfall if you got in trouble?

_____

_____

_____

5. (John 4:6–19) What was Jesus' overall attitude toward the woman at the well?

_____

_____

_____

6. Even if you might want to pray for and minister to her, do you think she would have been a good influence on you, your son, or your daughter?

_____

_____

_____

7. (Esth. 5:9–14) Whose lives would Haman have destroyed if he'd been able to bring about his evil plans?

_____

_____

_____

8. (1 Cor. 5:1–5) Why was Paul so concerned about the Corinthian Christian who'd been sleeping with his father's wife? Wouldn't that be a private matter?

_____

_____

_____

9. (1 Kin. 11:3) What effect did the sheer number of Solomon's wives probably have on his ability to rule wisely?

_____

_____

_____

10. (Gen. 4:23) Why was Lamech so proud of himself? What kind of person must he have been?

_____

_____

_____

11. (2 Sam. 11:1–26) David sinned badly but repented wholeheartedly and regained God's favor. Knowing that, would he have been a good friend to have in spite of his failures?

_____

_____

12. (Matt. 25:1–13) Without declaring the foolish virgins as *good* or *bad* people, would their willingness to serve the bride be a sufficient reason to want them for friends, despite their foolishness? Why or why not?

_____

_____

_____

FRIENDSHIPS THAT PRODUCE NEGATIVE RESULTS

Let us now take a look at one of the more fascinating characters in the Bible—fascinating in a negative way, unfortunately—and see what we can learn from the story of her partnership with a man she influenced in all the wrong ways. Many centuries have passed since this woman was thrown out of an upstairs window to her death, but she has not been forgotten. In fact, the name *Jezebel* has become synonymous with impudence, shamelessness, and a total lack of any morality or restraint.

However, Jezebel's story isn't the primary focus of this narrative for this exercise. She married a weak man named Ahab, one of the kings of Israel who is better-known than most because of his association with her, but a man with almost no moral compass of his own. Unfortunately, Ahab did not have much in the way of a role model in his immediate background. Of Ahab's father, Omri, the Bible tells us that "Omri did evil in the eyes of the LORD, and did worse than all who were before him" (1 Kin. 16:25 NKJV).

The Bible also tells us the same thing about Ahab, which means that the progression must have gone from bad to worse. However, it seems clear that Ahab's own weaknesses, his own willingness to sin, were themselves made worse by his marriage (and presumed "friendship") with Jezebel. During the course of their life together she had a tremendous impact on him.

Let's concentrate on that aspect of the story. The following short Scriptures highlight the Ahab/Jezebel story. Please fill in the blank spaces and then answer the questions.

Ahab is introduced in 1 Kings 16:30–33:

> Now Ahab the son of Omri did evil in the sight of the LORD, more than all who were before him. And it came to pass, *as though it had been a trivial thing for him to* _____ *in the sins of Jeroboam* the son of Nebat, that he took as wife Jezebel the daughter of Ethbaal, king of the Sidonians; and he went and served Baal and _____ him. Then he set up an altar for Baal in the temple of Baal, which he had built in Samaria. And Ahab made a wooden image. *Ahab did more to* _____ *the* LORD *God of Israel to anger than all the kings of Israel who were before him* (NKJV, italics added).

Jezebel came from a Phoenician port city called Sidon, where her father was a king in his own right. Sadly, the Sidonians worshiped both Baal and Asherah (called "Ashtoreth" in some translations), and Jezebel pushed and pulled Ahab in that direction as soon as they were married. Indeed, when Jezebel became queen, she immediately tried to eliminate her competition by massacring all the prophets of the LORD. However, a godly man named Obadiah hid 100 prophets in two caves and kept them alive on bread and water.

Eventually, in the middle of a horrific drought, while searching the desert for livestock feed, Obadiah encountered Elijah and sent him on to meet with Ahab. Their encounter is recorded in 1 Kings 18:17–19:

> Then it happened, when Ahab saw Elijah, that Ahab said to him, "Is that you, O _____ of Israel?"
>
> And he answered, "I have not troubled Israel, but you and your father's house have, in that you have _____ the commandments of the LORD and have followed the Baals. Now therefore, send and gather all Israel to me on Mount Carmel, the four hundred and

fifty prophets of Baal, and the four hundred prophets of Asherah, who eat at Jezebel's table" (NKJV).

In other words, between the two of them, Ahab and Jezebel supported 850 false prophets of Baal and Asherah (also another name for *Astarte,* from which we get the word "Easter").

🔆 (BREAKOUT) STRAIGHT FROM THE BOOK . . .

Each of us is moving in one direction or the other at any given time— either we are moving toward fulfillment of our fleshly desires without regard to God's wisdom, or we are moving toward God's way, plan, and purpose. Which direction is easier?

Next came the direct result of the command Elijah issued to Ahab in the passage above (imagine, a mere prophet commanding a king!), which resulted in the dramatic "Elijah and God against the world" confrontation. In this instance the Lord demonstrated His perfect sovereignty over all the universe, by inspiring Elijah to directly challenge the prophets of Baal to a contest to see whose God could actually do something "impossible."

Ahab and Jezebel's prophets prayed to their false gods from morning till noon. Then they cut themselves until the blood flowed freely, danced about their altar, and prophesied until evening. But their gods couldn't coax a single ribbon of flame from the driest of kindling wood.

Finally, Elijah's turn came. First Kings 18:38, 39 tells what happened after Elijah made the whole thing even more spectacular by drenching everything on the altar with water before he prayed to the *true* God:

Then the fire of the LORD fell and _____ the burnt sacrifice, and the wood and the stones and the dust, and it _____ _____ the water that was in the trench. Now when all the people saw it, they fell on their faces; and they said, "The LORD, He is God! The LORD, He is God!"

And Elijah said to them, "Seize the prophets of Baal! Do not let one of them escape!" So they _____ them; and Elijah brought them down to the Brook Kishon and _____ them there (NKJV).

When Ahab told Jezebel all that Elijah had done, she immediately sent him a letter promising to do precisely the same thing to him. She never got the chance, however, because he immediately ran away and went into temporary hiding. (And for doing so, by the way, God immediately admonished him and reminded Elijah of who he had on his side protecting him.)

Not too long after that, Ahab decided he'd like to have a certain vineyard that was close to his house, but it was owned by a man named Naboth who refused to sell. Ahab took to his bed, pouting, until Jezebel found him and asked what was wrong. First Kings 21:6–10 continues the saga:

He said to her, "Because I spoke to Naboth the Jezreelite, and said to him, 'Give me your _____ for money; or else, if it pleases you, I will give you another vineyard for it.' And he answered, "I _____ _____ give you my vineyard."

Then Jezebel his wife said to him, "You now _____ authority over Israel! Arise, eat food, and let your heart be cheerful; I will give you the vineyard of Naboth the Jezreelite."

And she wrote letters in Ahab's name, sealed them with his seal, and sent the letters to the elders and the nobles who were _____ in the city with Naboth. She wrote in the letters, saying, _____ a fast, and seat Naboth with high honor among the people; and seat two men, scoundrels, before him to bear witness against him, saying, You have _____ God and the king. Then take him out, and _____ him, that he may die.

101

Then, in verses 15, 16:

> And it came to pass, when Jezebel heard that Naboth had been
> _____ and was dead, that Jezebel said to Ahab, "Arise, take
> _____ of the vineyard of Naboth the Jezreelite, which he
> refused to give you for money; for Naboth is not alive, but dead." So it
> was, when Ahab heard that Naboth was dead, that Ahab got up and
> went down to _____ _____ of the vineyard of Naboth
> the Jezreelite (NKJV).

The next day, God sent Elijah to that same vineyard to give Ahab the following message. (1 Kin. 21:21–24):

> "Behold, I will bring _____ on you. I will take away your
> _____, and will cut off from Ahab every male in Israel, both
> bond and free. I will make your house like the house of Jeroboam the
> son of Nebat, and like the house of Baasha the son of Ahijah, because
> of the _____ with which you have provoked Me to anger, and
> made Israel sin.' And concerning Jezebel the LORD also spoke, saying,
> "The dogs shall _____ Jezebel by the wall of Jezreel.' The
> dogs shall eat whoever belongs to Ahab and dies in the city, and the
> birds of the air shall eat whoever _____ in the field" (NKJV).

✣ (BREAKOUT) STRAIGHT FROM THE BOOK . . .

There are no perfect friendships because there are no perfect people. There are, however, mature, godly, mutually rewarding and satisfying friendships—and those friendships tend to be ones in which both parties are seeking to become mature, godly, wise people.

Ahab put on sackcloth and repented immediately, which bought him a little more time. Eventually Ahab disguised himself, went to a battle at Ramoth, and was hit by an arrow meant for someone else and died. Later, as the servants were washing his bloodstained chariot, the dogs came and licked up his blood, fulfilling Elijah's prophecy in 1 Kings 21:19:

> And you shall speak to him, saying, "Thus says the LORD: 'In the place where dogs licked the blood of Naboth, dogs shall _____ your blood, even yours'" (NKJV).

Meanwhile, Jezebel's life had already come to an even sorrier end. After a series of would-be kings fought and eliminated each other, Jehu (the one left standing), came to Jezreel, spotted Jezebel in a window upstairs, and ordered those with her to end her life, (1 Kin. 9:32–35):

> And he [Jehu] looked up at the window, and said, "Who is on my side? Who?" So two or three eunuchs _____ _____ at him. Then he said, "Throw her down." So they threw her down, and some of her blood _____ on the wall and on the horses; and he _____ her underfoot. And when he had gone in, he ate and drank. Then he said, "Go now, see to this accursed woman, and bury her, for she was a king's daughter." So they went to bury her, but they found no more of her than the skull and the feet and the palms of her hands (NKJV).

1. Even though Jezebel's people were Baal/Ashtoreth worshipers and Ahab was an Israelite who should have worshiped the God of Israel, which of these two people appeared to be influencing the other the most?

_____

_____

_____

2. Regardless of the question of morality, which one had the stronger personality?

_____

_____

3. Would that have been considered normal or desirable in that era? Would it be considered desirable from God's point of view?

_____

_____

_____

4. Of all these events from the Ahab/Jezebel story, which one most decisively shows the inner workings and dynamics of their relationship?

_____

_____

_____

5. What useful suggestion might you want to offer Ahab—other than not marrying Jezebel in the first place?

_____

_____

_____

❇ (BREAKOUT) THE JEZEBEL SPIRIT

For hundreds of years, ministers of the gospel have warned against embracing and encouraging the "Spirit of Jezebel" within their churches and congregations. Indeed, Christ Himself, in Revelation 2:20, said: "Nevertheless I have a few things against you, because you allow that woman Jezebel, who calls herself a prophetess, to teach and seduce My servants to commit sexual immorality and eat things sacrificed to idols."

All the above is a measure of how powerfully the story of Jezebel grabs hold of our imaginations. More important, it's also a measure of how wicked she was. What exactly is this *Spirit of Jezebel*?

Perhaps the best way to define her is to examine what she actually did. Whether or not she seduced Ahab into marrying her is speculation. However, by allying herself with him she vastly increased her sphere of influence and her store of treasure.

Next, Jezebel promised to kill Elijah if she ever got her hands on him. She did have Naboth killed, and she undoubtedly would have killed anyone else who got in her way. Whenever it seemed expedient, she cheated, probably stole, was a priestess who served a false god, and literally helped lead millions of Israelites astray. She certainly had no prohibitions against immorality of every possible kind.

Even in dying she did things her own defiant way, putting on heavy makeup and arranging her hair just before being thrown from an upstairs window to her death below.

Is there any personal sin Jezebel might *not* have been willing to embrace to get what she wanted? A Jezebel Spirit is generally defined today as a spirit of extreme narcissism—tremendous selfishness and deceit that promote unrest.

EVEN A GOOD FRIENDSHIP CAN HAVE A NEGATIVE IMPACT

No matter how positive your liking for someone can be, even a strong friendship can have a negative impact. Without question, your friends in their humanity can disillusion and distress you, drag you down, and even destroy you if you give them enough power and authority over you.

It doesn't have to be that way, however.

Words to Remember . . .

Do not trust in a friend; Do not put your confidence in a companion; Guard the doors of your mouth from her who lies in your bosom. For son dishonors father, daughter rises against her mother, daughter-in-law against her mother-in-law; a man's enemies are the men of his own household (Mic. 7:5, 6 NKJV).

CLOSING PRAYER . . .

Our Father, we pray that You would help us to choose our friends carefully, guided only by Your wisdom, that we might be blessed through the company we keep. And may we also learn to be good friends ourselves, to bless those who bless us. And most of all, to bless You and praise Your name above all.

In Jesus' name, Amen.

CHAPTER SEVEN

WISDOM FOR BUILDING DEEP, LASTING, GODLY FRIENDSHIPS

In the previous chapter we spent quite a bit of time on potentially *negative* aspects of friendship. Our goal was to identity character traits and behavior patterns you would *not* want to bring into your life on purpose—influences you would be better off *not* to have too close.

None of that discussion, by the way, should discourage you from seeking to help anyone who might come to you with problems of a negative nature. However, you should be very careful about allowing them too much influence in your life. And sometimes, certain people can only be helped by specialists or people with considerable experience. It is never our responsibility to try to cure everyone else's ills on our own.

However, loving and wise fathers and mothers never send their sons and daughters out into the world without making them aware of what they are likely to encounter. Indeed, much of the Book of Proverbs contains exactly that kind of advice. A significant portion of Proverbs is concerned with things to avoid, contrasted with things to actually do, in order to live a life characterized by godly wisdom.

> ⚎ (BREAKOUT) STRAIGHT FROM THE BOOK . . .
>
> No man can ever meet all the needs in any woman's life.
>
> No woman can ever meet all the needs in any man's life.
>
> No friend can ever meet all the needs in any friend's life.
>
> But the good news is this: The Lord Jesus Christ can meet all the needs in your life so that you are better able to minister to and befriend another person.

Let's discern things you *should* look for in building friendships that will improve not only your life but the lives of your friends as well.

TEN WAYS TO BUILD WISE, GODLY FRIENDSHIPS

Let's begin by linking some basic characteristics of healthy, positive friendships with solid biblical illustrations. The first list below includes ten characteristics fundamental to healthy Christian friendships—the kinds that glorify God, build us up in all the important ways, and help us walk more wisely with God. Each characteristic is followed by a blank space.

Each item in the second list is followed by a Scripture reference that, in a few cases, contains quite a few verses. Many of these will already be familiar to you, but I would encourage you to look them up and reread them anyway.

Your challenge is to decide which characteristic each person in the second list exemplifies and then to write the correct names in the blank spaces in the first list. Some items might fit into more than one blank, but ultimately you should have an even match.

1. Shared faith in Christ Jesus   _____

2. Mutual interests   _____

3. Willingness to give more than receive   _____

4. Willingness to risk pain or rejection   _____

5. Vulnerability to each other   _____

6. An attitude of service   _____

7. Willingness to forgive freely and quickly   _____

8. Acceptance of both criticism and praise   _____

9. An adherence to biblical principles   _____

10. Proven over time   _____

James	(Entire Book of James)
Stephen, at his death	(Acts 7:60)
The poor widow and her mites	(Mark 12:41–44)
Early Christians	(1 Pet. 3:8, 9)
Paul	(2 Cor. 11:24–27)
Elijah, after Mount Carmel	(1 Kin. 19:9–15)
Moses	(Ex. 2 — Deut. 34:6)
David/Nathan	(2 Sam. 12:1–13)
Simon (Peter) and Andrew	(Matt. 4:18–20)
Mary and her vial of perfume	(Matt. 26:7)

If you think of others who would be equally good illustrations of the ten characteristics, add them to the list.

EIGHT BASIC BUILDING BLOCKS FOR DEEP FRIENDSHIP

Next, let's consider some of the building blocks that go into building solid, lasting friendships that glorify God and help you walk in His wisdom. If you are part of a group, this exercise might be a private one. Either way, the objective is to list the people in your life with whom you maintain friendships. These friends could include a husband, a wife, or a child—they do not have to be non-relatives. Even though the table below contains room for only five people, you could easily list several more.

> ❊ (Breakout) Straight from the Book . . .
>
> Casual friendships may seem to just happen. True, long-lasting, deep friendships, however, are built. They are established on a commonality of purpose and values; they are built through shared experiences and conversations marked by vulnerability and transparency.

Ultimately, the goal of the exercise is not a score of any kind. Rather, it's an honest evaluation of the friendships that currently surround you. Don't rate them in terms of positives or negatives. Instead, let this exercise tell you, at a very basic level, *where you might be able to improve* the quality of your friendships.

Building Blocks	Person #1	Person #2	Person #3	Person #4	Person #5
Time					
Talk					
Shared tears and laughter					
Expressed thankfulness					
Thoughtful gestures					
Tolerance					
Touching					
Transparency					

A FRIENDSHIP FOR THE AGES

When most Christians think of biblical friendships, the one they most often remember is the friendship between David and Jonathan, and there's a good reason. Let's look at a few Scriptures that illustrate various aspects of that famous friendship. Read the Scriptures, fill in the blanks as we go along, and then answer the questions.

> Now when he [i.e., David, after beheading Goliath] had finished speaking to Saul, the soul of Jonathan was knit to the soul of David, and Jonathan _____ him as his own soul. Saul took him that day, and would not let him go home to his father's house anymore. Then Jonathan and David _____ a covenant, because he loved him as his own soul. And Jonathan took off the robe that was on him and gave it to David, with his _____, even to his sword and his bow and his belt (1 Sam. 18:1–4 NKJV).

❖ (BREAKOUT) SALT COVENANT

Salt covenant is one of four ancient Hebrew covenants mentioned in the Bible but not fully explained. Those who were writing the original text, and those to whom it was first given, already intimately knew the concepts. Unfortunately, many modern Christians do not.

Salt covenant was also known as "friendship" covenant. It was a lifetime-and-beyond commitment, meaning that when one party died the survivor was obligated to do whatever he could to help that person's family. This, of course, explains why David searched out Mephibosheth (Jonathan's surviving son) after Jonathan's death, brought him into his own house, and honored him as one of his own sons.

Salt covenant derives its name from the way in which it was established.

People of that era, living in the desert and knowing something about heat-stroke, usually carried small bags of salt. It was not the refined salt of today, of course; rather, it was rocklike and yellow. The parties to the covenant would empty their salt bags into a common bowl, mix it all together, and then refill their bags from the mixture. From that day forward, the only way to cancel the covenant would be to return each of those grains of salt to their original owners, which, of course, was impossible. Thus, salt covenant could not be broken.

Frequently, the parties to the covenant would also exchange weapons and armor, as David and Jonathan did, plus other items of clothing as well. This exchange was considered one more way of expressing high regard for each other and sealing the agreement.

These verses signify the beginning of the friendship between David and Jonathan. (See "Salt Covenant" elsewhere on this page for more details). It's obvious, however, that the text greatly compresses the action. For the souls of these two young men to be "knit together" in friendship would require at least a short getting-to-know-you period.

The next selection regarding Jonathan and David details the first mention of Saul's growing obsession with killing David and eliminating someone Saul felt might someday be a rival for the throne. In the days immediately following David's defeat of the giant Goliath, Saul asked David to pursue other military options against the Philistines, which David dispatched with amazing skill for one so young. These maneuvers increased his already immense popularity with the Israelites, but in Saul's mind, David's successes quickly became a source of even greater anxiety, suspicion, and jealousy. The women of Israel were even singing songs in praise of David, comparing him to Saul—and Saul was losing the comparison battle.

We resume the biblical narrative with Jonathan's first recorded defense of David in front of his father: (1 Sam. 19:1–5)

Now Saul spoke to Jonathan his son and to all his servants, that they should _____ David; but Jonathan, Saul's son, _____ greatly in David. So Jonathan told David, saying, "My father Saul seeks to kill you. Therefore please be on your guard until morning, and stay in a secret place and hide. And I will go out and stand beside my father in the field where you are, and I will speak with my father about you. Then what I _____, I will tell you."

Thus Jonathan spoke well of David to Saul his father, and said to him, "Let not the king sin against his servant, against David, because he has not _____ against you, and because his works have been very good toward you. For he took his life in his hands and killed the Philistine, and the LORD brought about a _____ _____ for all Israel. You saw it and rejoiced. Why then will you sin against innocent blood, to kill David without a cause?" (NKJV)

In the next biblical account of David and Jonathan talking together, David is obviously frustrated. He does not mention the word *fear*, but it certainly would be reasonable to impute a little of that to him. David was being forced into extreme caution. The two men remained fast friends in spite of the tension surrounding them. In fact, Jonathan makes it clear once again that he will honor his original covenant commitment to David: (1 Sam. 20:1–4)

Then David fled from Naioth in Ramah, and went and said to Jonathan, "What have I done? What is my _____, and what is my sin before your father, that he seeks my life?"

So Jonathan said to him, "By no means! You shall not _____die! Indeed, my father will do nothing either great or small without first _____ me. And why should my father hide this thing from me? It is not so!"

Then David took an oath again, and said, "Your father certainly knows that I have _____ _____ in your eyes, and he has said, "Do not let Jonathan know this, lest he be grieved.' But truly, as

the LORD lives and as your soul lives, there is but a step between me
and death."

So Jonathan said to David, "Whatever you yourself desire, I will do
it for you" (NKJV).

⚜ (BREAKOUT) STRAIGHT FROM THE BOOK . . .

No person is strong all the time.
No person is correct all the time.
No person is perfect all the time.
And no person says just the right things all the time.

Next, in 1 Samuel 20:5–11, David is the one who voluntarily reaffirms their
covenant and even suggests that Jonathan should kill him himself if he (David) is
found truly guilty of any iniquity.

And David said to Jonathan, "Indeed tomorrow is the New Moon, and
I should not fail to sit with the king to eat. But let me go, that I may
hide in the field until the third day at evening. If your father
_____ me at all, then say, "David earnestly asked permission of
me that he might run over to Bethlehem, his city, for there is a yearly
sacrifice there for all the family.' If he says thus: "It is well,' your servant will be safe. But if he is very angry, be sure that _____ is
determined by him. Therefore you shall deal kindly with your servant, for you have brought your servant into a covenant of the LORD
with you. Nevertheless, if there is iniquity in me, _____
_____ _____, for why should you bring me to
your father?"

But Jonathan said, "Far be it from you! For if I knew certainly that
evil was determined by my father to come upon you, then would I not
tell you?"

Then David said to Jonathan, "Who will tell me, or what if your father _____ you roughly?"

And Jonathan said to David, "Come, let us go out into the field." So both of them went out into the field (NKJV).

✹ (BREAKOUT) THE COMING OF THE NEW MOON

The "new moon meal" with King Saul, to which David alluded in First Samuel 20:5, was an important observance to the ancient Israelites. In those times they established dates with great care so they could correctly observe the festivals as God had commanded them (Lev. 23:1–44). They literally recalibrated their calendars several times each year, based on each appearance of the new moon. In this way they could all agree on where they were in the year, what was coming next, and how many days away the next significant event might be.

Each new moon was officially established when at least two reputable witnesses testified before the rabbis in Jerusalem that they had seen the first sliver of moon in what had been a moonless sky. Each witness had to appear separately to avoid any hint of collusion, and the testimony of each one had to corroborate the other as to the precise location and appearance of the moon. Once these details had been established to the satisfaction of the rabbis, they offered sacrifices, burned incense, chanted special prayers, ate special meals, and blew their ram's horn trumpets (*shofars*) in jubilant celebration.

They also communicated the news to outlying communities through a system of signal fires that began on the hilltops of Jerusalem. Surrounding communities then built their own signal fires on their *own* hilltops, as did the communities lying farther and farther away from Jerusalem, until the entire nation of Israel was "on the same page" as we would say today.

The same system of signal fires, which also included the blowing of shofars, was used to establish the correct times for other important events as well. Because much of the resulting wave of light would then flow from Jerusalem to the communities to the west, all the way to the Mediterranean Sea, it's easy to see why some scholars believe that Christ's own words, "as the lightning comes from the east and flashes to the west" (Matt. 24:7), refers to this simple but effective way of keeping all the Israelites coordinated to observe the same dates for each 24-hour period.

In response, Jonathan reaffirms his commitment to David's safety. He then details the famous plan whereby he proposes to warn David of Saul's intentions by pretending to shoot his bow at a target and then speaking certain "coded words," to be overheard and deciphered by David, to the lad who retrieves his arrows: (1 Sam. 20:12–23)

Then Jonathan said to David: "The LORD God of Israel is witness! When I have _____ out my father sometime tomorrow, or the third day, and indeed there is good toward David, and I do not send to you and tell you, may the LORD do so and much more to Jonathan. But if it pleases my father to do you _____ , then I will report it to you and send you away, that you may go in safety. And the LORD be with you as He has been with my father. And you shall not only show me the kindness of the LORD while I still live, that I may not die; but you shall not cut off your kindness from my house forever, no, not when the LORD has cut off every one of the enemies of David from the face of the earth." So Jonathan made a covenant with the house of David, saying, "Let the LORD _____ it at the hand of David's enemies."

Now Jonathan again caused David to vow, because he loved him; for he loved him as he loved his own soul. Then Jonathan said to David, "Tomorrow is the New Moon; and you will be missed, because your seat will be empty. And when you have stayed three days, go down quickly and come to the place where you hid on the day of the deed; and remain by the stone Ezel. Then I will shoot three arrows to the side, as though I shot at a target; and there I will send a lad, saying, "Go, find the arrows.' If I expressly say to the lad, "Look, the arrows are on this side of you; get them and come'—then, as the LORD lives, there is _____ for you and no harm. But if I say thus to the young man, "Look, the arrows are beyond you'—go your way, for the LORD has _____ _____ _____. And as for the matter which you and I have spoken of, indeed the LORD be between you and me forever" (NKJV).

This conversation is followed by several verses detailing how Jonathan did exactly as he promised, warning David that—as David feared—Saul still had every intention of killing David by any means at his command. Verses 41, 42 from the twentieth chapter of First Samuel give us the last recorded interchange between David and Jonathan:

> As soon as the lad had gone, David arose from a place toward the south, fell on his face to the ground, and bowed down three times. And they kissed one another; and they _____ together, but David more so. Then Jonathan said to David, "Go in peace, since we have *both sworn in the name of the LORD, saying, "May the LORD be between you and me, and between your descendants and my descendants, forever."'* So he arose and departed, and Jonathan went into the city (NKJV, italics added).

The italicized portion reiterates both the existence and the terms of the eternal friendship covenant between Jonathan and David and between their descendants. David honored his covenant with Jonathan through Jonathan's son, Mephibosheth. Few documented friendships in all of history have been so genuine, so pure, so poignant, and such an outstanding example of what friendship should be about.

Likewise, few friendships (if any) have ever been so important to the history of the Jewish people—indeed, to the lineage of Jesus Christ Himself. Except for Jonathan, at a certain point there might not have been a David to both anger and delight the Lord in later years.

✺ (BREAKOUT) STRAIGHT FROM THE BOOK . . .

Don't expect a friendship to be instantaneous.

Don't expect a friendship to last forever with no effort on your part.

Don't expect a friendship to be so resilient that you can ignore it, abuse it, or devalue it without causing damage to the friendship.

1. Which of the ten *wise, godly ways to build friendships* (introduced at the beginning of this chapter) did David and Jonathan exemplify in their relationship?

_____

_____

_____

2. Which of the eight *"Basic Building Blocks for Deep Friendship"* (also introduced earlier in this chapter) did David and Jonathan build on in their relationship?

_____

_____

_____

3. Explain how and why you would credit any of the building blocks to them.

_____

_____

_____

The Impact of a Good Friendship on Your Life

The following three closing thoughts come from chapter six of *Walking Wisely*:

1. A friendship can delight you.

2. A friendship can develop you.

3. A friendship can drive you to excellence.

Absolutely.

Words to Remember . . .

David arose from a place toward the south, fell on his face to the ground, and bowed down three times. And they kissed one another; and they wept together, but David more so. Then Jonathan said to David, "Go in peace, since we have both sworn in the name of the LORD, saying, 'May the LORD be between you and me, and between your descendants and my descendants, forever'" (1 Sam. 20:41, 42 NKJV).

Closing Prayer . . .

Our Father, we pray that You would teach us not only to make good friends but to be good friends ourselves. As always, may Your wisdom guide us in this important aspect of our lives, just as we have asked You to guide us in all other things as well.

In Jesus' name, Amen.

CHAPTER EIGHT

WISDOM FOR HEALING A DAMAGED RELATIONSHIP

A friend of mine recently included the following in an e-mail on current events in his family:

> We're looking for a new car to replace the Beetle. Our lease comes up in a month or two. We have the option of buying it, of course, but now that we've moved out of the mountains and back to the flatland I don't think we want it anymore. Now we need a "road" car!

The "Beetle" in question, naturally, was a Volkswagen, one of the newer models that reappeared in the mid-90s. Another of my friends calls them "Roger Rabbit" cars because they look like something out of a cartoon—much more fun than the original VW Bug and a lot bigger as well.

The Beetle story actually illustrates something about friendships. That VW Beetle was a great car for driving mountain roads in the winter. It had high clearance, big tires for its overall size, a wide wheelbase for stability, and an engine positioned over the drive wheels for maximum traction.

> ### (BREAKOUT) STRAIGHT FROM THE BOOK . . .
>
> The plain and simple truth is this: Not all friendships are intended to last forever. Some are . . . and some aren't.

In other words, it was the right car for the right time for the right reason.

On the other hand, it was not a lifetime car, perfect for every situation. Other cars are bigger, roomier, and more comfortable for long-distance and freeway driving: that's the kind of vehicle my friends acquired when they turned in the VW.

FRIENDS FOR A REASON OR A SEASON

Friendships can be a little like automobiles in the sense that they aren't all suitable for all situations or for all times.

- For example, sometimes God sends a particular friend to you for a particular reason. Suppose you're having trouble doing something as mundane as filling out some insurance forms. So you go to the company's office, get some help, begin to like the way the person helping you talks and discover that he or she goes to a church much like yours; you have coffee once or twice, enjoy each other's company and appreciate the help, but then realize, three months later, that the "friendship" is basically over. The two of you still have warm regard for each other and will probably always remain casual acquaintances, but you have nothing in common strong enough to bring you together on a regular basis.

- Or, suppose you meet someone you really get along with in your sophomore year at college. In your junior year the two of you room together, and by the time you are seniors you have met each others' families, helped each other through English composition, calculus, and a required class in German. By then, of course you have become fast friends—lifetime buddies, as you both agree.

A few months later you graduate and go back to your hometowns, 1,500 miles apart. You get married and your friend is part of the wedding; then the exact opposite happens and you reciprocate. Ten years later you suddenly realize that it's been more than nine years since the two of you talked on the phone or saw each other in person. Unbelievable! Then you think about it and realize that you were just friends for a season—that you moved on to separate lives, grew in different directions, lost contact, and are now friends in memory only.

✵ (BREAKOUT) DISCERNMENT AND FRIENDS FOR A REASON

The word "discernment" comes up frequently in discussions of wisdom from God's perspective. Indeed, the words *discern* or *discernment* appear about thirty times in most translations of the Bible. The *first* example occurs in the 41st chapter of Genesis when Joseph interprets Pharaoh's dreams and advises him to "select a discerning and wise man, and set him over the land of Egypt" (v. 33) to deal with the famine God was about to bring upon the land. This very truth—what to do about the coming famine—was given by God to Joseph and thus was *discerned* through godly wisdom.

It seems that we cannot have godly wisdom without discernment, as Paul makes very clear hundreds of biblical pages later when he uses this meaningful word in its *last* appearance in the Bible:

> But the natural man does not receive the things of the Spirit of God, for they are foolishness to him; nor can he know them, because they are spiritually discerned (1 Cor. 2:14 NKJV).

On the physical level we can all think of examples of the differences between "seeing" and "discerning." For example, when you and I look at a man burning up with fever, shaking like a leaf, and barely able to stand up, we see "sickness." Yet a trained medical doctor, considering all those symptoms together with his knowledge of the man's history and the diseases common to his environment, might instantly discern "cholera," or "swamp fever," or something else entirely.

Now consider *spiritual discernment* in the following two-part exercise. First, what might you discern as a *root cause* from observing the following examples? Choose from such basics as loneliness, character flaws, poor upbringing, genetics, or any others that you might consider appropriate.

1. A person struggling with an addiction to drugs . . .

_____

_____

_____

2. A person ruled by jealousy and anger . . .

_____

_____

_____

3. A person who feels unwanted, unloved, and without friends . . .

_____

_____

_____

4. A young person who is failing in school or an older person failing on the job . . .

_____

_____

_____

5. A person of any age being pressured to engage in improper sexual activities . . .

_____

_____

_____

Now, even more important, how could you be a friend for a reason in any of the numbered examples above and help the person involved overcome the problems? Write some possibilities in the spaces below.

_____

_____

_____

_____

_____

_____

_____

_____

_____

FRIENDS FOR A LIFETIME

On the other hand, friendships for a lifetime are clearly of a different character and often of a different caliber as well. A 60- or 70-year friendship between two married people is a perfect example. Somewhat more rare, perhaps, might be a friendship between two men or two women, or less often a man and a woman, extending from grade school (or even before) straight through until one or the other passes away. A friendship like that could last 90 years or more!

> ⁂ (BREAKOUT) STRAIGHT FROM THE BOOK . . .
>
> If you do not want to restore your damaged relationship, do your best to end the relationship in peace. If both of you are withdrawing from each other, it may be that you can simply let the matter lie. If one person wants to sustain and repair the relationship, however, and the other person does not, you are going to find yourself in conflict.

To get an overall perspective on a whole series of biblical friendships, consider the friendship combination in the first column of the following table. Look up the Scriptures to review some of the details of the friendships and then put check marks in the last three columns if they were Friends for a Reason (F/R), Friends for a Season (F/S), or Friends for a Lifetime (F/L). ("Lifetime," of course, would be defined as beginning when the people involved became friends and ending when one passed away.) You might also indicate the length of each friendship, if it were of a known duration.

Please note that the Scripture references, in some cases, were too numerous to be listed separately, so the first and last verses in which both parties were mentioned are listed: for example, the disciples and Christ. Bits and pieces of their friendship are spread out over several chapters.

When you are finished with the table (and please feel free to add any examples you might think of), answer the questions that follow.

RELATIONSHIP	LENGTH	SCRIPTURES	F/R	F/S	F/L
The Disciples and Christ		Matt., Mark, Luke, John			
Paul and Barnabus		Acts 13:1—15:36			
Priscilla and Aquilla		Acts 18:2–26			
David and Jonathan		1 Sam. 18:1, 2 Sam. 21:7			
Joseph and his Brothers		Gen. 37:2—45:4			
Moses and Joshua		Ex. 17:9—Deut. 32:44			
Paul and Silas		Acts 15:22—18:5			
Jephthah and Elders of Gilead		Judges 11:1–11			
Boaz and Ruth		Ruth 2:1—4:17			
Balaam and Balak		Num. 22:1—24:25			
Philip and the Ethiopian		Acts 8:26–39			
David and Michal		1 Sam. 18:17—2 Sam. 6:23			
Rahab and the Spies		Josh. 2:1—6:25			
Ruth and Naomi		Ruth; all four chapters			
Solomon and Queen of Sheba		1 Kin. 10:1–13			
Daniel and the King		Dan. 6:6–28			
Nehemiah and Artaxerxes		Nehemiah 2:1–10			
Mary, Martha, Jesus, Lazareth		John 11:1–43			

1. Can you think of any *Friendships for a Reason* that you've had in your own life? List them below and identify the reason for which the friendship existed.

_____

_____

_____

_____

_____

2. Do the same for any *Friendships for a Season* you have also had and identify the season during which the friendship existed.

_____

_____

_____

_____

3. Do the same for any *Friendship for a Lifetime* . . .

_____

_____

_____

_____

(BREAKOUT) STRAIGHT FROM THE BOOK . . .

Nothing that is contrary to God's commandments can build up a friendship.

ATTITUDES AND BEHAVIORS THAT STOP THE FLOW OF LOVE IN A RELATIONSHIP

The goal of this exercise is to reconsider the series of biblical friendships you characterized as "for a reason, season, or lifetime." This time, think about the attitudes and behaviors that might have been part of the interaction between the parties to the friendship. Use the following list of attitudes and behaviors and write their corresponding numbers beside the characters' names.

For example, the relationship between Joseph and his brothers was certainly characterized by (3) jealousy, (5) explosive emotional behavior, (6) covetousness, and others as well.

(1) Selfishness

(2) Manipulation

(3) Jealousy

(4) Criticism

(5) Explosive emotional behavior

(6) Covetousness

(7) Premarital sexual intimacy

(8) Betrayal or disloyalty

The Disciples and Christ   _____

Paul and Barnabus   _____

Priscilla and Aquilla   _____

David and Jonathan   _____

Joseph and his Brothers   _____

Moses and Joshua   _____

Paul and Silas   _____

Jephthah and Elders of Gilead   _____

Boaz and Ruth   _____

Balaam and Balak   _____

Philip and the Ethiopian   _____

David and Michal   _____

Rahab and the spies   _____

Ruth and Naomi   _____

Solomon and Queen of Sheba   _____

Daniel and the king   _____

Artaxerxis and Nehemiah   _____

Mary and Martha   _____

Jesus and Lazarus   _____

WHEN A RELATIONSHIP FALTERS

Inevitably, some of your friendships will fall on rocky ground. When that happens, you have to decide whether they are worth saving or whether they were friendships for a reason or a season and are better left alone—not so much to die as to subside—and free up all parties to pursue other friendships and activities.

However, when you know in your heart that maintaining a faltering friendship would be a *good* and *proper* thing to do, the four *Action Steps* listed below occur in most situations. Each one is also Bible-based, although modern terminology might not be so easily found in the Scriptures.

We have few clear examples of faltering friendships in the Bible in which any of the parties did any of these four things, but that doesn't mean we can't think of *any*. For example, Joseph definitely implemented Action Step #4 by moving forward past any remaining bitterness when his brothers came back into his life.

Even though this exercise might be more difficult than some, let's bring back our list of biblical friendships *one more time*. Directly below are four action steps. Directly below *those* is the listing of the biblical friendships. This time, the goal is to indicate which (if any) of the four action steps were undertaken by any of the involved parties. Be aware that you will encounter at least three possibilities.

You might be surprised at what you discover as you consider these friendships one more time.

THE ACTION STEPS

STEP #1: Apologize to each other.

STEP #2: Identify constructive positive steps each can take. Deal in specifics. Focus on observable, definitive behaviors that can be readily done in the near future.

STEP #3: Make a mutual commitment to rebuild the relationship.

STEP #4: Agree to move forward and deal with the past as appropriate.

The Disciples and Christ _____

Paul and Barnabus _____

Priscilla and Aquilla _____

David and Jonathan _____

Joseph and his Brothers _____

Moses and Joshua _____

Paul and Silas _____

Jephthah and Elders of Gilead _____

Boaz and Ruth _____

Balaam and Balak _____

Philip and the Ethiopian _____

David and Michal _____

Rahab and the spies _____

Ruth and Naomi _____

Solomon and Queen of Sheba _____

Daniel and the king _____

Artaxerxis and Nehemiah _____

Mary and Martha _____

Jesus and Lazarus _____

✣ (BREAKOUT) TAKING PRIVATE STOCK

(You may want to do this exercise privately if you are using this workbook in a group setting. If you then wish to share with others, do so with discretion and discernment.)

1. By now you should have listed all the friendships you've enjoyed during your lifetime, according to various types. Do you see any kind of pattern? If so, describe it on the following page.

   _____

   _____

   _____

2. Does the evidence suggest that you have managed your friendships poorly or well—up to this point?

   _____

   _____

   _____

3. What changes, if any, would you like to make in the future?

   _____

   _____

   _____

4. Based on your study throughout this workbook and the book it complements, what would be the most effective, godly way for you to go about making desirable changes?

   _____

   _____

   _____

HEALING CAN BE STRENGTHENING

Some final thoughts, almost straight from the book, are appropriate at this point.

Nothing we have said or done in these pages, or in these exercises, should change the fundamental reality that *you should cherish and value each **type** of relationship, and each **individual** relationship, that you have enjoyed throughout your life.*

On the other hand, moving into the present and beyond, if you are still faced with deciding whether to walk away or to try to maintain a weak or faltering friendship, perhaps the following list will help. These are some of the basic signs, indicating that a relationship—however godly it might still be—has fallen upon hard times and needs to be reassessed, then reinvigorated or simply allowed to fade away peaceably. Relationships are impaired or harmed when

- you stop spending time together;
- you stop talking to each other;
- you become reluctant to share your sorrows and your joys—you stop crying together and laughing together;
- you no longer express your thanks or do thoughtful things for each other;
- you become increasingly critical of each other—less and less tolerant of each other's errors, less appreciative of each other's efforts, less accepting of each other's weaknesses;
- you stop touching each other with warmth and tender affection;
- you build a wall and no longer share your life freely with each other—one or both of you hold things back and conceal your motives, feelings, and thoughts;
- one or both of you lie to each other—not only about what you are doing, but what you are thinking and feeling with regard to your relationship;
- you stop trusting each other.

May all of the principles and examples we have touched upon in this chapter help you walk *more wisely and more closely with God* as you deal with the friendships that adorn your life!

WORDS TO REMEMBER . . .

Entreat me not to leave you, Or to turn back from following after you; For wherever you go, I will go; And wherever you lodge, I will lodge; Your people shall be my people, And your God, my God. Where you die, I will die, And there will I be buried. The LORD do so to me, and more also, If anything but death parts you and me" (Ruth 1:16, 17, NKJV).

CLOSING PRAYER . . .

Our Father, we pray that You would help us build and maintain godly friendships to Your glory. We also pray for the wisdom and discernment we need to rebuild relationships when they become damaged. May we walk always in Your wisdom and do all things accordingly. In Jesus' name, Amen.

(BREAKOUT) STRAIGHT FROM THE BOOK . . .

Work at reconciliation with the hope and the intent that your relationship will be more vibrant, more resilient, more mutually beneficial, and more purposeful. What God heals, God uses to bring glory to His name.

(BREAKOUT) WHAT WAS BEHIND THE RELATIONSHIP BETWEEN RUTH AND NAOMI?

Most Christians are familiar with the words of Ruth to Naomi, quoted in the "Words to Remember" section of this chapter. Many of us have at least a small sense of the depth and breadth of Ruth's devotion to Naomi—in other words, of the integrity of their friendship.

However, when we look at their relationship through ancient Hebrew eyes, and especially when we give equal consideration to what Naomi said to Ruth before Ruth made her oft-quoted "whither thou goest" reply, we get a fresh appreciation for what these two women actually meant to each other.

In that time and place, an older woman without a husband or sons would have no one officially charged with taking care of her in her old age. The New Testament widow who gave the tiny mites at the temple was a classic example. Likewise with the woman whose son God revived through the prophet Elijah. Her only remaining jar of oil continued to pour out its bounty long after it should have been empty, for God does take care of His own.

In addition, the New Testament provides numerous admonitions, directly from both Christ and His apostles, to "take care of the widows and orphans." This was long considered to be the most fundamental form of godly charity.

With that in mind, the words Naomi spoke to Ruth seem especially poignant and worthy of remembrance:

> But Naomi said, "Turn back, my daughters; why will you go with me? Are there still sons in my womb, that they may be your husbands? Turn back, my daughters, go—for I am too old to have a husband. If I should say I have hope, if I should have a husband tonight and should also bear sons, would you wait for them till they were grown? Would you restrain yourselves from having husbands? No, my daughters; for it grieves me very much for your sakes that the hand of the LORD has gone out against me!" (Ruth 1:11–13 NKJV)

CHAPTER NINE

WISDOM IN TIMES OF CONFLICT AND CRITICISM

I once knew a husband and wife who had entirely opposite personalities. To me and to most of their other friends, Nancy always seemed flighty, spacey, and impossible to pin down. In twenty years I never heard her give an opinion on anything, and I never saw her be in charge of any aspect of the home she shared with Tom. Sometimes we wondered who kept the place clean and who was responsible for their three charming, well-mannered, very bright kids.

Tom, of course, was the bottom-liner. He ran his own business, earned all the money, picked out all the cars, and made all the other major decisions. He was a rock, a crusher, a genial guy who wore a huge smile but always had an agenda. Nowadays we might call him a linear thinker—a guy whose mind always went straight ahead and never turned off.

Then one day, one of his customers filed a large lawsuit against Tom's company. The issue was not a moral one at all; Tom was not being accused of anything unethical, illegal, or even unscrupulous. He was simply named as the party responsible for what happened when a product he designed and developed caused a lot of harm.

In a matter of weeks, Tom frayed around the edges so much that some of us hardly recognized him. Gone was the confident strut and hearty greeting. In its place came glazed eyes and a lot of mumbling.

Then one day, he and Nancy went to visit his mother and found her lying on the floor in a pool of blood. Tom totally lost control. He couldn't even dial the phone; Nancy had to yank it out of his hand to call 911. He was even too distraught to follow the ambulance to the hospital. In more than thirty years of marriage he had always been the driver everywhere they went. But this day he sat in shock as Nancy took over.

In the weeks ahead, Tom's mother passed away from her injuries, resulting partly from a stroke and partly from hitting her head when she fell. Her death, of course, meant that her estate had to be dealt with, and Tom had been named executor in her will. However, he couldn't deal with it, so Nancy did.

Neither could he make any funeral arrangements; that fell to Nancy, too, as did calling the family and bringing everyone together for a week-long reunion that literally changed several lives in profound ways.

Most amazing of all, however, was what all her friends thought of as "Nancy's transformation." Things were never quite the same after that, and I'm not talking specifically about the loss of their loved one or the eventual legal judgment against Tom's company. The legal difficulties hindered him a bit and caused him to make some design changes, but eventually all those problems went away.

No—I'm talking about the simple fact that Tom had never allowed Nancy to take any kind of a lead in anything they did together, until he had no choice. What most people thought of as Nancy's lack of ability was simply Nancy's lack of opportunity—*and lack of necessity.*

❈ (Breakout) Straight from the Book . . .

Conflict is part of every person's life. It is found at home, work, school, in the neighborhood, between friends, at sports arenas, and yes, even in the church. We can't escape conflict. Rather, we need to learn how to deal with it and respond to it. In nearly all cases, conflict, misunderstanding, and criticism go together, at least to a degree.

❈ (Breakout) Jesus Laid It Down

From time to time, someone will write or speak about "Christly behavior." Usually their points are well taken, yet often Christ's behavior at His own trial is held up as an example for all of us to follow.

His humility in that situation certainly can serve as an example, but in one very important sense we cannot use Christ's behavior at that phony "trial" as a model for all circumstances. Christ was not really "on trial" for His life. A trial presupposes the best evidence available from both the prosecution and the defense. In His case the prosecution fabricated much of their evidence, but even that is not the point.

As Christ Himself said, "No one takes it [His life] from Me, but I lay it down of Myself. I have power to lay it down, and I have power to take it again. This command I have received from My Father" (John 10:18 NKJV).

If Christ had not been purposely laying down His life for us, He undoubtedly could have mounted a defense that would have made His accusers look very foolish (actually, He did some of that anyway). Also, as the old, once-popular hymn says, He could have called 10,000 angels.

Therefore, His refusal to respond to His accusers' accusations has to be taken as what it was—not "giving up" but "giving over." Christ was not "losing" His life but volunteering to sacrifice it.

In other words, Christ's behavior in all other cases is a model we should always try to emulate, but in this unique case it is not a perfect model for how *we* should behave when *we're* falsely confronted or falsely accused. Certainly His behavior when He drove the moneychangers out of the temple indicates that Christ did not believe in utter passivity in every circumstance, and certainly not when the honor of His Father was at stake.

We Christians have the same rights and obligations to defend ourselves as anyone else has. The difference is that we are further obligated to act in wisdom and humility, with God's help, when we are confronted with falsity.

MANAGING CONFLICT AND CRISIS

Necessity might be the mother of invention, but when it is combined with conflict and crisis, it often becomes a catalyst for something more. In the language our friend Tom once used, sometimes all three of these factors working together "blow people in or blow people out." It doesn't matter whether we're talking about business, a personal crisis, or your relationship with God.

Let's first concentrate on personal crises for one simple reason. If you can manage relationships on a personal level, by learning to rely on the wisdom of God, you'll develop the underlying resources you need to manage things on a larger level.

Twelve short passages from Scripture, followed by the main characters involved in each one, are listed below. Below each listing are four questions pertinent to the passage:

1. **First,** who was the offending party in the conflict or crisis the Scriptures refer to or describe? Were both sides of the conflict responsible, or was there just one culprit?

   (If the answer is not obvious, read a few verses before and after the particular passage to help you understand the passage.)

2. **Second,** what was done, by anyone at all, to manage the conflict and resolve it in a healthy way? Was *anything* done? Were attempts at resolution one-sided or mutual?

3. **Third,** what would *you* have done if you'd been the offended person? What if you'd been the offender?

4. **Fourth,** how do you think Christ Himself might have resolved each of these situations if he'd been the innocent party? Where there was *no* innocent party (meaning roughly equal responsibility on both sides of the issue), how might He have counseled the participants?

GENESIS 39:19, 20 — POTIPHAR'S WIFE AND JOSEPH

1. Offending Party? _____

2. What was done to resolve the problem?

   _____

   _____

   _____

3. What would you have done?

   _____

   _____

   _____

4. What would Christ have done?

   _____

   _____

   _____

_____

GENESIS 27:1–41 — ESAU AND JACOB

1. Offending Party? _____

2. What was done to resolve the problem?

_____

_____

_____

3. What would you have done?

_____

_____

_____

4. What would Christ have done?

_____

_____

_____

GENESIS 30:1, 2 — RACHEL AND JACOB

1. Offending Party? _____

2. What was done to resolve the problem?

_____

_____

_____

3. What would you have done?

_____

_____

_____

_____

4. What would Christ have done?

_____

_____

_____

ESTHER 1:9–21 — AHASUERUS AND VASHTI

1. Offending Party? _____

2. What was done to resolve the problem?

_____

_____

_____

3. What would you have done?

_____

_____

_____

4. What would Christ have done?

_____

_____

1 SAMUEL 17:28 — ELIAB AND DAVID

1. Offending Party? _____

2. What was done to resolve the problem?

_____

_____

_____

3. What would you have done?

_____

_____

_____

4. What would Christ have done?

_____

_____

_____

1 SAMUEL 20:30 — SAUL AND JONATHAN

1. Offending Party? _____

2. What was done to resolve the problem?

_____

_____

_____

3. What would you have done?

_____

_____

4. What would Christ have done?

_____

_____

_____

1 SAMUEL 20:34 — JONATHAN AND SAUL

1. Offending Party? _____

2. What was done to resolve the problem?

_____

_____

_____

3. What would you have done?

_____

_____

_____

4. What would Christ have done?

_____

_____

_____

2 SAMUEL 12:5 — DAVID AND NATHAN

1. Offending Party? _____

2. What was done to resolve the problem?

_____

_____

_____

3. What would you have done?

_____

_____

_____

4. What would Christ have done?

_____

_____

_____

JUDGES 14:12–19 — SAMSON AND MEN OF TIMNAH

1. Offending Party? _____

2. What was done to resolve the problem?

_____

_____

_____

3. What would you have done?

_____

_____

4. What would Christ have done?

_____

_____

_____

GENESIS 4:4–7 — CAIN AND ABEL

1. Offending Party? _____

2. What was done to resolve the problem?

_____

_____

_____

3. What would you have done?

_____

_____

_____

4. What would Christ have done?

_____

_____

_____

GENESIS 31:36 — JACOB AND LABAN

1. Offending Party? _____

2. What was done to resolve the problem?

_____

_____

_____

3. What would you have done?

_____

_____

_____

4. What would Christ have done?

_____

_____

_____

GENESIS 34:1–31 — SIMEON AND LEVI VERSUS SHECHAM AND THE HIVITES

1. Offending Party? _____

2. What was done to resolve the problem?

_____

_____

_____

3. What would you have done?

_____

_____

_____

4. What would Christ have done?

_____

_____

_____

❖ (BREAKOUT) STRAIGHT FROM THE BOOK . . .

You can't help a person who doesn't want to be helped. You can't force a perfectionist to change his ways. You can't force a proud person to lay down his pride. You can't cause a person to seek healing for damaged emotions if that person doesn't want to be healed or sees no need for healing. You can't insist that another person lay down hatred, resentment, and bitterness. You can't require another person to forgive. And therefore, you can't change all causes of conflict or erase all criticism.

UNAVOIDABLE TRUTHS ABOUT CONFLICT

No matter what your intentions might be in any given situation, conflict even among God-fearing people cannot always be avoided. Three guidelines about conflict have proven true over and over again:

1. Even though conflict cannot always be avoided,

2. all conflict is not sin. Even so,

3. conflict among equals is not inevitable.

The Bible says, "As iron sharpens iron, so a man sharpens the countenance of his friend" (Prov. 27:17 NKJV). However, some people routinely respond to conflict in three unhealthy ways:

1. They *suppress* their feelings and deny the impact the conflict is having on them. They fail to heed their emotions by denying them or dismissing them completely.
2. They *repress* their feelings. They acknowledge the conflict, but they refuse to express their feelings or their opinion. Rather, they keep quiet in the hope that it will go away by itself.
3. They *blame and accuse others* rather than accepting any responsibility for either causing or resolving the conflict.

The four most common causes of the above behaviors are

1. a failure in communication;

2. emotional baggage and projection;

3. perfectionism; and

4. pride.

Let's look at what a person *could* do in response to a conflict rather than suppressing, repressing, or blaming and accusing and then justifying *that* action with failures in communication, with emotional baggage, with projection, with perfectionism, and with pride. *Instead of all that,* consider

TEN HEALTHY, RIGHTEOUS WAYS TO DEAL WITH CONFLICT

1. Refuse to respond in anger.

2. Make no attempt to defend yourself immediately.

3. Ask the Holy Spirit to put a seal on your lips and to put a guard on your mouth. Make your prayer in a time of conflict the prayer that David prayed:

> Set a guard, O LORD, over my mouth; Keep watch over the door of my lips (Ps. 141:3).

4. If after calm reflection you still find yourself totally puzzled as to what created a conflict, ask the Holy Spirit to reveal the cause.

5. Regardless of how a conflict arises, see the conflict from God's perspective.

6. Ask the Holy Spirit, "Is this my fault?"

7. Forgive the other person.

8. As soon as possible, begin to treat the other person with genuine kindness and tenderness.

9. Choose to learn something from the conflict. Ask the Holy Spirit, "How can I avoid a conflict such as this in the future?"

10. View the conflict as an opportunity to respond as Christ would respond.

Finally, let's put these ten ways of dealing with conflict in a useful context by familiarizing ourselves with ways to use them in real life. Recognize that God will give additional insights when you walk in wisdom with Him. Begin by considering the following examples. Using the ten ways to resolve conflict, indicate two things: **First,** identify the unhealthy way that the person in the example responded. **Second,** identify the righteous way(s) that the same person *could* have chosen to respond which *might* have defused or resolved the conflict before it got serious.

Examples:

1. You are in charge of a large department within the company you work for. You have an employee who sometimes seems needlessly contentious. He also has a slight hearing loss. One day you ask him to take care of a certain task, well within his job description. Instead, he goes to the human resources manager and files a complaint against you for an improper racial slur. What do you do?

   _____

   _____

   _____

   _____

2. You are the first person in the checkout line at the grocery store. Just as the clerk reaches for your first item, another woman dashes in front of you, throws five items down on the counter, and says, "Please! I'm in a big hurry!" Immediately, all 13 people behind you raise an uproar. "Hey! Don't let her do that to us!" they all cry as one. The checker, rather than taking charge, is intimidated and looks at you with a big question mark in her eyes. What do you say or do?

   _____

   _____

   _____

   _____

3. You are cut off on the freeway by a woman driver with a wild look in her eyes, obviously drunk, deranged, or frantic about some emergency. She almost kills you and several others, but finally gets in front of you and is hidden by other cars. Moments later you spot her pulling into a rest stop, bouncing on a flat tire. You have plenty of time to pull over and offer to help. What do you do?

   _____

_____

_____

4. You are sitting in your living room at home behind a window that screens you from sight from outside. You spot someone you've never seen before walking a big dog. He stops right in front of you. The dog sniffs in your fresh-mowed yard and then leaves a deposit so quickly you can't react. What do you do now?

_____

_____

_____

_____

5. You are just leaving your office. Suddenly, a person you don't know very well, from another part of the office, asks to speak to you. When you agree, she tells you about a conversation she overheard between your boss and another person who does essentially the same job you do, but on different projects. Supposedly, he is telling her he wants her to completely redo the work you've just completed on a rush project that you put your heart and soul into. What do you do next?

_____

_____

_____

_____

6. You buy a car and the salesman promises you a free CD player, to be installed as soon as the new stock comes in. Two weeks later, you visit the dealership to make arrangements for the installation. The salesman you dealt with has been fired, and the company claims that it is not responsible for any verbal promises—only for what was written into the actual contract you signed. What next?

_____

_____

_____

7. Your best friend works for a computer manufacturer and is allowed to buy two computers at an employee's price far below anything you could equal anywhere else. Since you need a new one desperately, you agree to buy one through your friend. When it comes time to put up the money and complete the deal, your friend hems and haws and promises to deal with it later. That same day, through a second friend, you learn that the deal he promised to you he gave to someone else and probably doesn't know how to tell you that you were replaced. What do you do?

_____

_____

_____

_____

❖ (Breakout) Straight from the Book . . .

Not all conflict is rooted in willful behavior. Furthermore, conflict can result in something good.

A positive resolution of any conflict always starts with a choice.

Words to Remember . . .

Several Scriptures bear directly on what we've discussed in this chapter. The first is a longer passage from the Book of Nehemiah regarding the children of Israel and their frequent failures.

The second group of six short verses, which you might consider memorizing, comes from Proverbs or Ecclesiastes:

But they and our fathers acted proudly, hardened their necks, and did not heed Your commandments. They refused to obey, and they were not mindful of Your wonders that You did among them. But they hardened their necks, and in their rebellion they appointed a leader to return to their bondage. But You are God, ready to pardon, gracious and merciful, slow to anger, abundant in kindness, and did not forsake them (Nem. 9:16, 17 NKJV).

A soft answer turns away wrath, but a harsh word stirs up anger (Prov. 15:1 NKJV).

He who is slow to anger is better than the mighty, and he who rules his spirit than he who takes a city (Prov. 16:32 NKJV).

The discretion of a man makes him slow to anger, and his glory is to overlook a transgression (Prov. 19:11 NKJV).

He who sows iniquity will reap sorrow, and the rod of his anger will fail (Prov. 22:8 NKJV).

Wrath is cruel and anger a torrent, but who is able to stand before jealousy? (Prov. 27:4 NKJV)

Do not hasten in your spirit to be angry, for anger rests in the bosom of fools (Eccl. 7:9 NKJV).

CLOSING PRAYER . . .

Our Father, we put all our personal conflicts into Your hands, for Your help in resolving each one according to the lessons You have given to us. May we not be stiff-necked; may we not hide from the reality of conflict, and may we not be tempted to blame others when it comes. Instead,

*may we once again walk in wisdom with You and deal in righteous ways,
as You direct, with all that comes into our lives.*

In Jesus' name, Amen.

(BREAKOUT) FOR YOU ARE A STIFF-NECKED PEOPLE

The expression *stiff-necked* occurs twelve times in the *New King James Version* of the Bible. In all cases it was said of Israel—three times by the Lord, five times by Moses, once by David who was paraphrasing God (Ps. 75:5), and once each by Hezekiah, Jeremiah, and Stephen. What does it mean?

Our modern sense of it is that it means *obstinate* and *hard to work with*, but where does the expression come from? What is a truly stiff-necked person, anyway?

In biblical times, God encouraged the children of Israel to be herders and farmers. As such, they used oxen to do most of their plowing, for which they developed both single and double *yokes*, made of heavy pieces of wood, to go over the neck of each ox, fasten him to the harness, and rest against his shoulders so he could get all his muscle into the job.

When they were training a young ox to work in harness they would yoke him with an older, wiser, better-trained ox that would essentially keep the youngster in line and show him what to do. Occasionally they encountered a young ox that would bawl in rebellion and refuse to lower his head so he could be put in harness.

A stiff-necked person is one who refuses to put his head down, shut his mouth, and go to work.

Within the same example, of course (and assuming the old and young oxen could be linked together at all), comes the meaning of the phrase *unequally yoked*.

CHAPTER TEN

WISDOM FOR ESTABLISHING THE ULTIMATE RELATIONSHIP

Modern science has pretty much proven that it's impossible to kill two birds with one stone but only in a strictly literal sense involving real birds and a real rock. Let's think about that concept in an allegorical way.

When we are *saved*, we establish a true relationship with Jesus Christ by accepting His forgiveness of our sins. That acceptance is only the beginning. Up to that point, Christ has done ALL the work, and we have done nothing but accept His grace.

Most Christians understand this. On the other hand, many speak of then moving on to a new relationship with Him based on some of the criteria that is about to be introduced. First, a clarifying thought:

Eons ago, the moon was hung in the sky by God. It has always been the same moon, orbiting the same Earth. Moses looked at it; David looked at it; even Christ Himself looked at the same moon from our vantage point while He lived here on Earth.

⁂ (BREAKOUT) STRAIGHT FROM THE BOOK . . .

We need the Holy Spirit, whom Jesus sends to live in every believer. We need the Holy Spirit to guide us into the full truth about Jesus Christ. We need the Holy Spirit to direct our steps daily, and to help us make wise choices and godly decisions. We need the Holy Spirit to remind us of God's commandments and the truth of Jesus Christ so we will know what to do and what to say in any situation we find ourselves.

However, because of the positions and the movements of Earth and the moon, relative to each other, we see the moon in different phases that form repetitive patterns. And those patterns each take about a month to complete before the basic pattern starts again. In other words, it's not really a *new* moon that we see every month, even though we often use that expression. Instead, it's really a *renewed* moon.

So it is with our relationship with Christ. As that relationship develops, it is constantly renewed. As our commitment to Him deepens, we become more and more eager (and willing) to respond to His guidance—in summary, *walking wisely with God*, the main subject of this study. It involves moving through the typical phases of a constantly growing, ever-renewing relationship with Him.

That relationship is designed to last throughout eternity. It constantly changes, but it's never new in the sense that we ever want to think of laying it down and then starting a brand new one sometime later.

In other words, *The Ultimate Relationship* with God will always go through different fundamental phases:

1. The first phase of any ultimate relationship with God has to include accepting Jesus Christ as Lord and Savior.

2. The second phase of any such relationship has to include serving Jesus as our Lord.

3. The third phase of any such relationship has to include loving Jesus as our friend.

4. The fourth phase of any such relationship, not always included in a list as in the one above, includes inheriting eternal life when we pass from this life and begin eternity in His presence. Whether we are among the living when He comes back for His own, or whether we (like millions before us) will have to be resurrected from the dead, really doesn't matter. Eternity with Him is still assured.

> ### ❖ (BREAKOUT) STRAIGHT FROM THE BOOK . . .
>
> We need the Holy Spirit to comfort us when we experience pain and sorrow. We need the Holy Spirit to convict us of our sins and errors so we can repent and make positive changes in our lives. We need the Holy Spirit to defeat evil on our behalf. We need the Holy Spirit to conform us to the image of Christ Jesus.

Finally, our level of acceptance (our willingness to respond) determines our level of relationship with Jesus Christ. He is always willing to deepen His relationship with you. All He asks in return is that you be willing to take on more responsibility for deeper understanding and commitment and that you express that willingness through both prayer and actions.

Willingness in action equals a *closer walk*, just as *faith* in action equals *trust*.

HOW CAN YOU APPLY WHAT YOU KNOW ABOUT THE ULTIMATE RELATIONSHIP?

Let's look at several biblical illustrations of these points. There are several Scripture passages, followed in each case by the main *subject* of each passage, followed by four columns labeled *Phase #1*, *Phase #2*, *Phase #3*, and *Phase #4*. Your challenge is to read each text and then put a check mark in the remaining columns to indicate which of the four phases in the *Ultimate Relationship* it illustrates.

Of course, one example could easily illustrate more than one phase, but try to base your decisions *not on what you know about that person or event* but, rather, on what the Bible *clearly says* within the passage in question. Then answer the questions that follow the table.

SCRIPTURAL PASSAGE	SUBJECT	PHASE #1	PHASE #2	PHASE #3	PHASE #4
Matthew 4:18–20	Calling of Peter and Andrew				
Acts 9:1–6	Paul, on the Road to Damascus				
John 3:1–21	Nicodemus, hearing Christ				
Luke 23:39–43	Thief on the Cross				
Acts 13:42–48	Gentiles, believing in Christ				
Acts 18:1–4; 24, 25	Aquilla and Priscilla (totality)				
John 11:1–40	Resurrection of Lazarus				
Matthew 9:9	Calling of Matthew				
John 19:26; 20:2; 21:20	The apostle John (various)				
Luke 5:17–20	Paralyzed man				

1. Is it always easy to determine the level of commitment of these people in their personal walk with the Lord?

_____

_____

_____

2. Do any of these stories suggest that it's possible to skip Phase #1? If so, which one(s)?

_____

_____

_____

3. If you believe that the correct answer to (2) above is "no," do you then agree that the phases of your relationship with Christ have to be entered in the order stated at the beginning of this chapter?

_____

_____

_____

4. At what phase are you at this very moment?

_____

_____

_____

5. If you are not at Phase #3, what do you believe you can do to attain that phase?

_____

_____

_____

HALLMARKS OF FRIENDSHIP WITH JESUS

Another way to look at the truths we've tried to illustrate above is to recognize the distinctive hallmarks of friendship with Jesus:

1. Sacrificial love, one-directional at first but which should eventually go both ways

2. An ongoing initiative by Him—He always reaches out (but we should do the same with others)

3. Revolutionary and positive change in us

4. His abiding presence, which never leaves us

Let's now see if we can illustrate each of the above hallmarks through the story of the apostle Paul. Paul has had an enormous influence on the fundamental doctrines of most of Christendom through his letters to churches at Rome, Ephesus, Corinth, and other cities—not to mention his letters to Timothy, Titus, and Philemon.

(Breakout) Straight from the Book . . .

Serving Jesus as Lord is all about obedience, submission of our will to His, being sensitive to His daily guidance, and being committed to fulfilling His will for our lives.

Paul might also be considered the ultimate example of one who is *not* all talk and no deeds. Paul lived everything he wrote about. It sometimes seems that he went through every hardship, frustration, misunderstanding, mistreatment, temptation, and spiritual agony known to man, yet he came out at the other side praising God and glorifying His name.

And to remain consistent, let's *not* quote Paul's own writings. Instead, let's look at the historical record only, as recorded in the Book of Acts. Therefore, in the spaces below there are four selections from Acts. The Scripture references are listed separately. Your challenge is threefold:

1. First, read the selections and then assign the correct scriptural addresses to each one in the space provided. Take the scriptural addresses from the list at the end

of the last selection. You might have to look some of these up, but try to do it first from memory—or dead reckoning—if you can!

2. Second, examine each selection carefully and assign one of the four *Hallmarks of Friendship* to each of the four selections. In other words, where was Paul in his walk with the Lord in each of the selections from the Book of Acts? You might have to adjust your assignments to use all four, but work it out so that they are all accounted for.

3. Third, as always, answer the questions that follow the selections.

In no particular order the selections include:

1. Then Saul arose from the ground, and when his eyes were opened he saw no one. But they led him by the hand and brought him into Damascus. And he was three days without sight, and neither ate nor drank.

   Now there was a certain disciple at Damascus named Ananias; and to him the Lord said in a vision, "Ananias." And he said, "Here I am, Lord."

   So the Lord said to him, "Arise and go to the street called Straight, and inquire at the house of Judas for one called Saul of Tarsus, for behold, he is praying. And in a vision he has seen a man named Ananias coming in and putting his hand on him, so that he might receive his sight."

   Then Ananias answered, "Lord, I have heard from many about this man, how much harm he has done to Your saints in Jerusalem. And here he has authority from the chief priests to bind all who call on Your name."

   But the Lord said to him, "Go, for he is a chosen vessel of Mine to bear My name before Gentiles, kings, and the children of Israel. For I will show him how many things he must suffer for My name's sake."

   And Ananias went his way and entered the house; and laying his hands on him he said, "Brother Saul, the Lord Jesus, who appeared to you on the road as you came, has sent me that you may receive your sight and be filled with the Holy Spirit." Immediately there fell from his eyes something like scales, and he received his sight at once; and he arose and was baptized.

Scriptural Address _____

Hallmark of Friendship _____

2. And a vision appeared to Paul in the night. A man of Macedonia stood and pleaded with him, saying, "Come over to Macedonia and help us." Now after he had seen the vision, immediately we sought to go to Macedonia, concluding that the Lord had called us to preach the gospel to them.

Scriptural Address _____

Hallmark of Friendship _____

3. Then the multitude rose up together against them; and the magistrates tore off their clothes and commanded them to be beaten with rods. And when they had laid many stripes on them, they threw them into prison, commanding the jailer to keep them securely. Having received such a charge, he put them into the inner prison and fastened their feet in the stocks.

But at midnight Paul and Silas were praying and singing hymns to God, and the prisoners were listening to them. Suddenly there was a great earthquake, so that the foundations of the prison were shaken; and immediately all the doors were opened and everyone's chains were loosed. And the keeper of the prison, awaking from sleep and seeing the prison doors open, supposing the prisoners had fled, drew his sword and was about to kill himself. But Paul called with a loud voice, saying, "Do yourself no harm, for we are all here."

Then he called for a light, ran in, and fell down trembling before Paul and Silas. And he brought them out and said, "Sirs, what must I do to be saved?"

So they said, "Believe on the Lord Jesus Christ, and you will be saved, you and your household." Then they spoke the word of the Lord to him and to all who were in his house. And he took them the same hour of the night and washed their stripes. And immediately he and all his family were baptized. Now when he had brought them into his house, he set food before them; and he rejoiced, having believed in God with all his household.

Scriptural Address _____

Hallmark of Friendship _____

(BREAKOUT) PAUL'S UNIQUE QUALIFICATIONS

Paul's unique experiences as a committed follower of Christ include beatings, stonings, imprisonments, hunger, and all the other physical and spiritual privations he endured.

Paul was also highly qualified to do the true work of the Lord once he accepted Jesus Christ as Lord and Savior because he was also a trained rabbi with a detailed, minute knowledge of the Scriptures. Indeed, he was one of the prized students of the well-known Pharisee scholar/teacher, Gamliel, who himself had been taught by the even better-known Hillel.

In other words, at a certain level, God's choice of Paul made sense. On the other hand, why did God choose someone who was spending every waking moment persecuting other Christians? For that matter, why choose Matthew as a disciple, a man who was one of the hated tax collectors of his era? Why Peter and Andrew, mere fishermen who had probably spent barely a day in school? Why not choose from the learned class, from the city fathers, from the doctors, lawyers, and accomplished doers of that era?

The answer seems to lie in the nature of God Himself. He truly seems to delight in "raising up" men and women of humility, people of honor and integrity to whom He can safely grant the wisdom and the knowledge they need to do His work. Many passages in Isaiah, Jeremiah, Ezekiel, and the Book of Proverbs bear this out, and it is also reinforced, near the very end of the Bible, by the words of both James and Peter:

> But He gives more grace. Therefore He says: "God resists the proud, but gives grace to the humble" (James 4:6 NKJV).

> Humble yourselves in the sight of the Lord, and He will lift you up (James 4:10 NKJV).

> Therefore humble yourselves under the mighty hand of God, that He may exalt you in due time . . . (1 Pet. 5:6 NKJV).

4. Then Saul [Paul], still breathing threats and murder against the disciples of the Lord, went to the high priest and asked letters from him to the synagogues of Damascus, so that if he found any who were of the Way, whether men or women, he might bring them bound to Jerusalem. As he journeyed he came near Damascus, and suddenly a light shone around him from heaven. Then he fell to the ground, and heard a voice saying to him, "Saul, Saul, why are you persecuting Me?"

And he said, "Who are You, Lord?"

Then the Lord said, "I am Jesus, whom you are persecuting. It is hard for you to kick against the goads."

So he, trembling and astonished, said, "Lord, what do You want me to do?"

Then the Lord said to him, "Arise and go into the city, and you will be told what you must do."

Scriptural Address _____

Hallmark of Friendship _____

Scriptural Addresses: Acts 16:9, 10; Acts 9:8–18; Acts 9:1–6; Acts 16:22–34 (Quotations are from the NKJV.)

1. Was there anything in Paul's (i.e., Saul's) background that qualified him for special status in God's eyes?

_____

_____

_____

2. Do you know of anything in his background that gave Paul special qualifications for doing the job God had in mind for him?

_____

_____

_____

3. Either way, do these Scriptures suggest that Paul's relationship with God featured the four Hallmarks of Friendship?

_____

_____

_____

4. Is there any reason to assume that *your* relationship with Him would *not* include those same four Hallmarks?

_____

_____

_____

5. Which Hallmark are you experiencing at this time in your life?

_____

_____

⁂ (BREAKOUT) STRAIGHT FROM THE BOOK . . .

Jesus chose to die for us out of His infinite, unconditional love for us. His life was not taken from Him—He purposefully and willfully laid it down in order that you and I might become His eternal friends (John 10:18).

In all possible respects, Christ is truly our ultimate *Friend of Friends*. What kind of friend are you to Him?

WORDS TO REMEMBER . . .

Are they Hebrews? So am I. Are they Israelites? So am I. Are they the seed of Abraham? So am I. Are they ministers of Christ? . . . I am more: in labors more abundant, in stripes above measure, in prisons more frequently, in deaths often. From the Jews five times I received forty stripes minus one. Three times I was beaten with rods; once I was stoned; three times I was shipwrecked; a night and a day I have been in the deep; in journeys often, in perils of waters, in perils of robbers, in perils of my own countrymen, in perils of the Gentiles, in perils in the city, in perils in the wilderness, in perils in the sea, in perils among false brethren; in weariness and toil, in sleeplessness often, in hunger and thirst, in fastings often, in cold and nakedness—besides the other things, what comes upon me daily: my deep concern for all the churches. Who is weak, and I am not weak? Who is made to stumble, and I do not burn with indignation? (2 Cor. 11:22–29 NKJV)

CLOSING PRAYER . . .

Our Father, may You grant us the willingness to deepen our relationships with You. May You also grant us the wisdom to recognize our constant need to move forward. May we never forget that walking in wisdom with You requires a never-ending, never-wavering, never-lessening com-

mitment on our part to be, to do, and to become all that we know You wish for each of us in Your perfect wisdom.

In Jesus' name, Amen.

✖ (Breakout) Wisdom and Understanding

Read the sentences below and then answer the questions that follow:

Understanding tells us *what* is happening—wisdom tells us *why*.

Understanding gives us the *facts*—wisdom tells us *what* to do and *how* to do it.

If you are familiar with the "Ws" of journalism—who, what, why, when, where, (and how)—do you see how *understanding* and *wisdom* relate to each other from the journalistic viewpoint?

Another oft-used word is *synergy*. When you have synergy, things are working together, and you get *more* than the sum of the parts.

God always rewards us in this fashion. In fact, was it not Jesus Himself, who said:

> Or what man is there among you who, if his son asks for bread, will give him a stone? Or if he asks for a fish, will he give him a serpent? If you then, being evil, know how to give good gifts to your children, how much more will your Father who is in heaven give good things to those who ask Him! (Matt. 7:9–11 NKJV)

NOTES

1 The "land of Shinar" was a flat plain in what is now Iraq. It eventually
became Babylonia; clearly, this piece of land has a long and storied history.

2 Some will say that this example from the Book of Samuel did not involve the
Holy Spirit, but was God the Father instead, because the Holy Spirit had not
yet been sent to dwell within us. Focusing on that particular fine point (accu-
rate or not) misses the larger one. God is one being with three equal parts
(Father, Son, and Holy Spirit), and each of those parts functions in complete
harmony with the others. As Christ Himself made clear so many times, He
came to do the will of the Father, as the Holy Spirit continues to do to this day
and as the Father Himself might very well have done in Old Testament times.

ABOUT THE AUTHOR

CHARLES STANLEY is pastor of the 15,000-member First Baptist Church in Atlanta, Georgia. He is the speaker on the internationally popular radio and television program *In Touch*.

Twice elected president of the Southern Baptist Convention, Stanley received his bachelor of arts degree from the University of Richmond, his bachelor of divinity degree from Southwestern Theological Seminary, and his master's and doctor's degrees from Luther Rice Seminary.

NOTES

NOTES

NOTES

Notes

NOTES

NOTES

NOTES

NOTES

Dr. Charles F. Stanley's series of Bible study guides feature insights and wisdom of this beloved pastor and author. Each title takes a unique fourfold approach to get the most out of Bible study time emphasizing personal identification with the Scripture passage, recognition of your emotional response, reflection of the passage's meaning and application, and taking steps to apply what's been learned.

Advancing Through Adversity (ISBN: 0-7852-7258-5)
Relying on the Holy Spirit (ISBN: 0-7852-7260-7)
Becoming Emotionally Whole (ISBN: 0-7852-7275-5)
Talking With God (ISBN: 0-7852-7276-3)
Listening to God (ISBN: 0-7852-7257-7)

Only
$7.99 Each

NELSON IMPACT
A Division of Thomas Nelson Publishers
Since 1798

www.thomasnelson.com

ARE YOU WALKING WISELY?

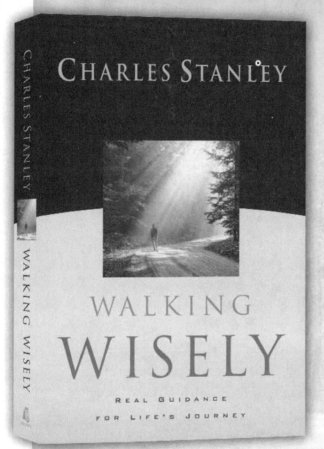

Dr. Charles Stanley cuts through the mystique of wisdom and presents God's simple plan to bless those who walk in His ways.

In Walking Wisely, bestselling author Dr. Charles Stanley reveals this simple fact: there are only two ways to journey through life . . . wisely or unwisely.

Those who walk wisely can expect to live a life of contentment and peace; a life overflowing with the confidence of God's love and presence. Those who walk unwisely can expect a life of conflict, disappointment, and discontent.

WHICH PATH HAVE YOU CHOSEN?

YOUR ENEMY IS STRONG.
THE BATTLE IS REAL.
PREPARE FOR VICTORY.

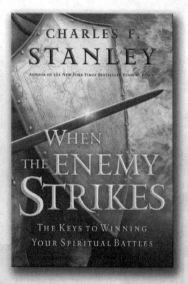

Fear, discouragement, loneliness, anger, temptation. These struggles are common to every human. Yet not all circumstances or negative emotions originate within. They could be the result of a willful, coordinated assault of Satan.

In *When the Enemy Strikes*, best-selling author Dr. Charles Stanley explores the often-overlooked reality of spiritual warfare—the tactics used by Satan to taunt, confuse, slander, and harm. Your adversary wants to crush your will, delay your promise, hinder your destiny, destroy your relationships, and lead you into sin. Dr. Stanley reveals how you should respond.

The battle is unavoidable, but take heart! God has given you the strength to stand.

NELSON BOOKS
A Division of Thomas Nelson Publishers
Since 1798

www.thomasnelson.com